AN
Only Child No More

Discovering My New Family at 54

MARTHA LEVALLEE

AUTHOR'S NOTE

This is a true story; however, the names of most of the people and some of the places have been changed. The writings from my father and from non-native speaking individuals have not been corrected for grammar, punctuation, spelling, etc. This pertains both to those from Germany writing in English, and me writing in German.

Contents

CHAPTER 1

How It Began

Although it started out as a weekday just like any other, it was actually the first day of a wonderful, unbelievable new chapter in my life. My story is proof that you never know what life has in store for you each day.

It was Wednesday, April 9, 2014, and I went to work later in the morning, as was my usual schedule on Wednesdays. I worked as an academic advisor for a small public college that caters to adult learners. My co-worker Billie was scheduled to conduct a workshop in our computer lab about our online courses later that afternoon. So she went to a scheduled career fair for high school seniors at the local community center for the first shift of the event, while I stayed back at the office. We then swapped places for the latter half of the event.

The career fair was held in the "cafetorium" of the small city's community center, a space used for feeding school-aged children that doubled as a gym and auditorium. The smells of slightly spoiled food, sour milk, and cleaning solution took me back to my days in public school after the lunch periods were over and the kitchen and janitorial staff worked on cleaning up.

I spent most of my time at the event watching the people. There were teens, some with a parent, who wandered to a couple of tables set up around the perimeter of the room. But most of the attendees ended up congregating back in the middle of the room, just chatting. It was obvious they had little interest in the jobs being offered by the local donut chain restaurant or the temp agency, or some of the other organizations with representatives present.

At the back of the room, a trickle of families came in to pick up their food allocations, as the room also functioned as a food pantry for the needy. One or two parents would walk in with their children in tow and exit with a box full of pantry items. A hopelessness clouded the atmosphere in the room; very few people came to my table to consider a local college. No other colleges were represented at the event, and many of these young people didn't show any interest in education beyond high school. These folks got by from day to day as best they could, but their futures seemed to hold few rainbows.

I thought to myself, "There, but for the grace of God, go I." I could relate to these people, as the small rural public schools I attended from grades one through twelve were half-filled with a similar population, with some middle-class and a smattering of slightly wealthier kids mixed in for good measure. I had been lucky that I was good in school, although I had to work very hard studying. My hard work had paid off, and I was able to graduate from college (using a great deal of financial aid), and even went on for my Master's degree and beyond. My mother encouraged my interest in school, reading to me as a child and "playing school" with me before I was old enough to attend. And my dad had often said to me "Get all the education you can." He didn't want me to drop out of school like he needed to, or have to work in factories like his brother and sisters did.

After a couple of hours, the event drew to a close, and I packed up the materials Billie had brought and returned to the campus office. After unloading the car, I went to my office and checked my emails. In my in-box were several messages, mostly from my students, but there was also one from a strange young man who said he was from Germany.

From: Samuel Graf
Sent: Wednesday, April 09, 2014 2:30 PM
To: Levallee, Martha
Subject: Research. I need your help

Dear Mrs. Levallee,
*   my name is Samuel, i am 26 and from Cologne, Germany. It might*

sound weird but i am looking for a man who was named Lawrence Rollins.

While researching i found your name connected to him. I might be totally wrong, but if so please please let me know. In this case i would explaine more to you.

This is no spam or anything, for me this is an incredible important research and you might be my only chance.

I hope you receive this mail and answer me.

Yours,
Samuel Graf
Cologne, Germany

At first, I thought it might just be spam that had made its way through the college's filters. I even printed off the email to show Billie after her workshop had ended and asked her, "If you were me, would you even bother to respond to this, or would you just throw it away?"

She looked at it and said, "I don't know – is that your father's name?" and I said yes it was, and it was spelled correctly also.

She said, "Go ahead; maybe you'll find out you have some relatives you didn't know about."

I laughed loudly as I walked down the hall back to my office, calling out "I don't think so," in a sing-song voice. That thought was just totally ludicrous to me. My father would never have been involved in something like that.

I debated for a few hours whether to respond to this email or not. I was intrigued that someone in a foreign country was doing research on my father. Daddy had been a blue-collar worker all his life, and to my knowledge he had never done much of anything during WWII that was particularly noteworthy. He had grown up as the middle child of five, and in a railroad depot, no less. My grandparents had been very young when they married in 1914, and they quickly had a daughter and then two sons within the first three and a half years of their marriage, with their younger two daughters coming along just a few years later. Grandpa worked as a fireman for the B&M Railroad, and Grammy ran the telegraph machine and sold tickets for the train. As part of their compensation they were able to (perhaps even expected to) reside in the depot. As adults, my father and his siblings would recount humorous tales of growing up in that railroad station. It was a miracle that none of the five kids were ever seriously hurt, as they played near the railroad tracks and hid in culverts. They were a poor family but made their own fun. Daddy hated school and quit at the end of ninth grade to go to work to help support the family.

My dad, Lawrence, and my mother, Rose, eloped in 1940, when she was eighteen and he was twenty-two, and he had a few different jobs in their early years of marriage. He entered the army in 1943, deciding shortly after Pearl Harbor that if he volunteered, maybe his older brother (who had a wife and child at that point) would be spared from the draft. There may have been no correlation, but his envisioned scenario worked out. My father was the only one of his parents and siblings who served in the military, and he was always very proud of that.

After returning from the service at the end of WWII, he bounced around from job to job, and finally landed work with the state's highway department. He was able to find his niche there, and eventually retired from the state. He never made a lot of money, but we always had plenty of food, a decent home, and adequate clothing (my mom sewing much of mine and most of her own). The thought of a foreigner believing that my father had done something noteworthy and doing "important research" about him seemed very enticing to me.

By the end of work that evening, I decided to go ahead and respond. My curiosity about why this strange young man was interested in my father was piqued. I cautiously wrote back:

Hello Samuel,
What is your research?
My father was Lawrence Rollins, now deceased.
                                    Martha (Rollins) Levallee

I continued to use my work email address, because I did not want to share anything personal with this stranger yet. I was still very suspicious of this being spam.

When I got home that evening, I told my husband about the strange email I had received. He agreed that it made sense to be suspicious and careful in my response.

CHAPTER 2

Who is Martha (Rollins) Levallee?

I guess I should tell you a bit about myself. I'm fifty-four, blonde but gray-ing, married to Eric for over twenty-five years, and usually a "glass-half-full" type of person. I have worked in higher education in New England for over three decades, but my career has had its ups and downs, as three of the colleges I worked at announced their impending closures while I was there. Thankfully I was able to successfully switch from one college to another in similar types of positions (registrar, academic advisor, campus director) without too much difficulty. Early on in this career, I had ambitions of becoming a college president, but after spending a day shadow-ing a woman who held the presidency of a small public college, I decided maybe this wasn't my dream job. I realized that I enjoyed working more directly with students.

I always loved school, and even liked to "play school" before I was old enough to attend, using a little desk with a chalkboard top. My mother, Rose, had encouraged this love of school and had been a good student herself; she even graduated from high school at fifteen years of age. While my parents knew that they could never afford to pay the significant costs of sending me to college, they did their best not to discourage my dreams of earning not only my Bachelor's degree, but also a Master's, and maybe even a PhD. Luckily, I graduated from high school in the late 1970s, when federal financial aid was plentiful for academically achieving students from families of lower and lower-middle incomes. I had always been "a nerd," and I enjoyed math and science, as well as music, and I spent many hours studying each week.

I had few childhood playmates, growing up in thickly-wooded Carterville as an only child. My hometown had lots of acreage of forestland, ponds, and fields, but little population. Luckily, I did have a first cousin once removed who was my same age, Tommy. He had an older sister, Lucy, who was just a couple of years older than us, and they lived in Carterville too. Occasionally I'd have play dates with them, and I saw Tommy every day in elementary school since we were in the same class. But these play dates were not as frequent as I would have liked. I was quite lonely as a kid; in fact, I longed for more regular playmates, or siblings.

My father was the middle of five children, and I sometimes pretended that I was his younger sister Gloria (my favorite aunt), way back in the late 1920s when they were all young children playing together. My imaginary playmates were my actual aunts, uncle and father, in their childhood. The fact that my grandparents had both worked for the B&M Railroad and lived in the Carterville Railroad Depot while raising their five children made this imaginary situation even more fun. I would pretend that travelers would come to our home and purchase train tickets, and "Ma" would yell at "us kids" for acting foolishly around the customers, just as I had heard my father and his siblings actually describe in their reminiscences.

My mom was a wonderful mother and growing up she was my best friend and confidant. Each afternoon after school, I would go home and relate my stories to her of what had happened in school that day while she cooked supper. This continued even after my Carterville Elementary School classmates and I were bussed to the next town for grades seven through twelve. My many hours of studying each evening and weekend paid off, as I was able to eventually graduate as Valedictorian of my small high school class, totaling fifty-three students from both towns. My good grades and extracurricular activities helped me get accepted to several colleges and get scholarships to afford attending.

But I never felt like I lived up to being "as good as Rose" in many respects, even though I was better at math than she was – she stopped being able to help me with my math homework when I got to algebra. But she was an accomplished pianist, and played piano and organ for various town functions as well as nearby weddings and funerals, and she acted as a substitute church organist. She was a good seamstress and made most of her own clothes, as well as mine, until my teenage years when girls focused on clothing brands and fit. And she was an excellent secretary, having been secretary to the bank commissioner of our state for many years prior to my birth. She was a whiz at typing and stenography. I took typing in my senior year of high school, but only so that I would be able to type my papers for college courses, and was never nearly as proficient as she. I didn't inherit her significant musical talent or sewing abilities. I struggled with my piano lessons, and often got frustrated that I didn't read music very well and had to learn new songs by ear. I wasn't very good at, and did not enjoy, sewing or knitting or crocheting or tatting, which my mother was able to do with such ease. My mother went to church most every Sunday, and her influence on me to "do my best and be my best" ran deep. I had her as a role model, which in almost all respects was great. But I always felt not quite good enough to measure up to her.

But my father was much more laid back, and I felt that he was very accepting of me. I was his pride and joy. Around the house he would often act silly to make me laugh. He would sometimes sing along with a song on TV, off-key in a falsetto voice. He liked comedy shows the best and would sometimes do a foolish little dance when Roy Clark played the banjo on *Hee Haw*. He spent many of his workdays driving around the state for his highway department job and would often pick up an inexpensive little trinket for me during one of his stops at a country store or market. Sometimes it was merely a pack of gum. Once he brought me a clear plastic dime bank that would hold $5 worth of dimes, and he told me I could spend the $5 on anything I wanted once I had saved that much. One year for my birthday (as a pre-teen) my parents gave me a cassette tape recorder so that I could record songs I liked from the radio. Occasionally my dad would record silly stories for me. I was very fortunate; my childhood home was full of much love and laughter.

Eric and I have been married for over twenty-five years, but never had any children. There were a variety of reasons for that. Part of it was because I very much wanted a fulfilling career, and I felt that having to take time off from that career to stay at home and raise young children would interfere with that goal. I had never been around babies and young children very much, and so I really wasn't very knowledgeable about them nor felt comfortable around them. But there was also another reason.

When I was in my early teens, my mother saw on the news that a particular anti-miscarriage drug that had been given to pregnant women in the late 1950s and early 1960s had recently been found to cause sterility in the baby girls who were born to those pregnant women. Rose was horrified and immediately contacted her doctor to find out if that particular drug was what she had been given when she had been pregnant with me. My mother had two miscarriages before giving birth to me, one in the early 1940s, after my parents had been married for only a year or so, and then another in the mid-to-late 1950s. So when she learned that she was pregnant for a third time, my mother wanted to do whatever she could to avoid miscarrying again. When her doctor suggested an anti-miscarriage drug, she agreed to take it. Then, well over a decade later, she feared that the drug she had willingly taken to make sure she carried her third pregnancy to term could mean that her daughter might never be able to have children of her own. My mother's doctor eased her mind a bit when he informed her that the particular anti-miscarriage drug from that study was *not* the one she had been given. However, he said that there were no similar studies done for the drug that she *had* taken, so there was really no way to know if a similar side effect was present or not. My mother then told me this information, and that because of all this, there was the possibility that I might not be able to have children. While this was not *good* news, I was not terribly concerned about it, as my goals emphasized career rather than motherhood. But the seed was planted in my mind at a rather early age that I might never have children even if I wanted them.

Eric and I met through mutual friends when I was twenty-six and he was thirty-one, and we hit it off right away, finding out that we had a lot in common. For one thing, we were both rather ambivalent about having children. And we were each an only child of older parents, and quite close with them. While we lived much nearer to his parents after we got married, he didn't mind at all that I wanted to make the two-and-a-half-hour round trip drive to visit my parents every couple of weeks. He got along well with them, especially my dad, who was more supportive and encouraging of Eric than his own father was. Eric is a "car guy" through and through, and although my dad didn't have as much extensive knowledge about autos as my husband, the two men would enjoy their discussions about auto mechanics and small engines and related topics. And Daddy showed Eric a few tips about woodworking. While some guys dread visiting their in-laws, Eric actually enjoyed our visits with my folks. He said that in many ways, he felt closer to his father-in-law than he did to his own father.

After we had been married for several years, we started to experience the death of our parents. My dad was the first one to pass away, which was not unusual, as he was the oldest of the four, and had smoked since his days in the army in the '40s. He had always said that he needed a way to stay awake on guard duty at night, and so he took up smoking. He succumbed to cancer in 1997, and spent his final few months in hospice care. Eric's mother suffered for many years with Alzheimer's disease, and she died from complications of it in 2006. When this took place and Rose didn't even send Eric a sympathy card, I realized that my own mother's mind was quickly fading. In her earlier years, she never would have forgotten to send a family member a sympathy card. Not long after the death of my mother-in-law, my mom admitted to me that she didn't know if she was taking her prescriptions correctly.

In May of 2007 – Mother's Day weekend to be exact – I was able to get my mother into an assisted living facility right there in Carterville, the town where she had lived most of her married life. Although both her doctor and I had had conversations with my mom about leaving the house where I had grown up to live somewhere safer than being alone, she didn't feel that relocating was needed quite yet. This was despite her having fallen several times while at home alone in 2005 and 2006, and even breaking her ankle in 2006. Ma's mental abilities continued to gradually diminish after she moved into the assisted living facility, evidently due to a later-identified heart issue that stemmed from the severe heart attack she experienced in 1994. She had hospice care for the final weeks of her life and passed away in November 2009.

When Eric's father passed away after a stroke in late 2012, Eric and I were both left with just cousins and a couple of distant aunts as our only remaining family. Some cousins we saw a couple of times per year, while others we rarely saw. Eric and I were each other's only immediate family, as our parents no longer existed, except in our memories. With no siblings and thus no nieces or nephews, and no children of our own, we really had no close family left. Now as middle age flies by, I sometimes find myself wishing for an adult child or two; young adults who are close enough family members that I could talk with and share things with on a regular basis.

CHAPTER 3

Who was Lawrence Rollins?

My father was the middle child of five, born to very young parents. My Grammy and Grandpa Rollins had only been in their teens when they got married and had their eldest child, Lucille. Grandpa worked for the B&M Railroad as a fireman, and he used a railcar to follow the trains to make sure no sparks caught the brush or grass or trees near the tracks on fire. When looking at an old photo of Grandpa, one of his great-grandchildren mentioned that he was so strong his arms looked like trees. Grammy used the telegraph machine in the railroad station to send and receive messages, and she sold tickets to passengers. The family lived in the depot as part of their employment, and the eldest four of their five children were all born right there in the station (their youngest child, Darlene, was born in a local hospital). The family was quite poor, but were a close-knit group. My dad was close to his older brother Harold growing up; they were only twenty-one months apart in age.

As adults, my father lived most of his life in Carterville, while elder brother Harold got a job at a large manufacturing organization on the other side of the state and raised his family there. The geographic distance and the expense of telephoning meant that the brothers were not as close as adults as they were as kids. Instead, Daddy grew closer to his two sisters who were nearest to his age—Lucille, who was a few years older, and

Gloria, who was a couple of years younger. As my Rollins grandparents aged and their health deteriorated, my father and his two sisters bore the brunt of the responsibility to care for them. Grandpa's dementia was particularly hard on Daddy, as his father had seemed so strong and invincible to young Lawrence growing up. I almost never saw my dad cry, but when he learned of his father's passing, that was one of those times. The other time I saw him wipe away tears was at Eric's and my wedding.

Because the family was quite poor with five growing mouths to feed, and my dad always disliked school, he quit in the ninth grade to go to work at a local farm to help support the family. His older brother and sister graduated from high school, but not Daddy or his younger siblings. This was a decision that he regretted later in life. But he never attempted to go back to school. He probably would have been diagnosed with a mild learning disorder if such things had been identifiable in rural America in the 1920s. His ability to read and write were less than perfect. He used to say to me as I grew up, "Get all the education you can." which I took literally and hoped to one day earn my PhD. But upon reflection, I think he just meant to complete high school, as that did not require additional personal expense. During most of his life, college was only available to rich kids, and thus he never thought his daughter would be able to attend college.

He and my mother Rose started dating when she was seventeen and he was twenty-one. At first, they ran into each other with friends, and would meet at a local fair, dance, or other social event. Many times I heard this story from either my dad or his siblings: When Daddy first went to call on my mother at the dairy farm where she lived with her parents and younger brother, it was Rose's *mother* – not Rose – who answered the door, much to his chagrin. My grandmother could be a rather stern woman, and in that moment, he was too nervous to ask to speak to Rose. So instead, he asked this dairy farmer's wife if he could purchase a pint of cream, pretending that was the purpose of his visit. The transaction took place, and he headed for home. But on the way, he wasn't sure how he would explain to his siblings why he had bought cream instead of seeing Rose. So, he decided to dispose of the cream… by drinking it. It wasn't long before Lawrence's digestive system caused him to regret that decision. He soon realized that being laughed at by his siblings for being "too chicken" to ask for Rose would have been the lesser evil than his decision to consume his purchase. Thankfully he soon got over his jitters about calling on my mother, and within a year they had eloped. It was obvious to me throughout my life that my mom and dad loved each other very much.

During my childhood, my dad had a stable job with the state's highway department, which did not require much overtime so he could spend evenings and weekends at home. He was a devoted husband and father. And he did what he could to provide a good life for us. But there was no money for luxuries like family vacations or for me to go to college. He would sometimes take my mother and me on day trips to the ocean or to a lake or to the mountains. Many times my mother would pack us a picnic lunch for such excursions, but occasionally we would eat out at a restaurant.

Occasionally my dad would mention to me, only half-jokingly, "Gee I sure hope that I can go to your high school graduation without needing a cane." Because my parents had been married for two decades before I came along, they were quite a bit older than most of the parents of my peers. I think he was trying to plant the seed in my mind that he wouldn't always be strong and healthy after I became an adult.

He had become "Uncle Lawrence" long before being called "Daddy." As a young adult, he had enjoyed bringing his sibling's children to local fairs, or on day trips to the mountains. Decades later his nephews and nieces still adored him, and would visit my parents regularly while I was growing up, either with their parents or alone. Those visits from my father's relatives were treasured times for me, filling our home with laughter. He and his brother would tease each other in their middle-aged years. "I've got a lot more hair than you have," my Uncle Harold would say to my dad, to which Daddy would reply, "Yeah, but I'm a lot better looking than you." Whenever his sister Gloria visited, there was always much laughter, and she made a particular point of paying attention to me. Lawrence's youngest sister, Darlene, sometimes struggled financially. She had a daughter, Paula, who was the same age as me. They lived a couple of towns away from us. Sometimes my dad would go out of his way to include Paula on our occasional bowling excursions, and when Paula and I were young children, there were a few years when Daddy would purchase a second Christmas tree to make sure that there was one in Darlene and Paula's home for the holiday.

His father had taught him some woodworking skills, as Grandpa had been a very good carpenter. My dad also got some training in the army and had helped to build bridges in Germany after the war was over. His "Enlisted Record and Report of Separation" indicates his honorable discharge and that his Military Occupational Specialty was "Carpenter Heavy Construction." His highest rank was T/5 and his listed decorations/citations included a Good Conduct Medal, a European African Middle Eastern Theater Campaign Ribbon, an American Theater Campaign Ribbon, an Army Occupation Medal, and a Germany Victory Medal. The section of the form for "Battles and Campaigns" listed simply "Rhineland Central Europe."

My dad's old army yearbook, *245 Engineer Combat Battalion - Its History and Achievements 1943–1945*, indicated that he had been part of A Company with the 245th Engineer Combat Battalion, and was activated in November 1943 at Camp Shelby, Mississippi. The following quotes are from the A Company section of that book:

"Up until March 6th we were taught everything that could possibly be given to a raw recruit during basic training.... It was shortly after this that we began making preparations for Tennessee maneuvers. March 13th we left Camp Shelby by truck convoy...Upon arrival in Tennessee, we traveled to Manchester and to Watertown, where the battalion C.P. [Command Post] was set up and the line companies were assigned to different sections of the maneuver grounds to repair all damage caused to the countryside by previously maneuvering troops. The work that we did included road repair, bridge constructions, culvert work and the operation of a stone quarry."

"August 10th brought us word that we were alerted for overseas duty, and for a month afterward we were busy creating TAT [To Accompany Troops] equipment and getting our personal affairs in order. The last we saw of Camp Shelby was on October 23rd, when we left by train for a P.O.E. [Point of Embarkation], which at that time was unknown to us. ......New Jersey and Camp Kilmer first came into our sight on October 25th......on October 29th we were hustled from Camp Kilmer to New York Harbor. Under the cover of darkness, we boarded the Staten Island ferry and got our first look at salt water, which we were to see for many days thereafter......We passed the Statue of Liberty at this time also. For many of us it was our first sight of the grand old lady, and for all of us it was to be our last sight for many months to come. Upon reaching Staten Island, we were treated to some popular music by a ... band and coffee and doughnuts served by the Red Cross, just before we boarded the U.S. Explorer. That night we were assigned sleeping quarters on the boat, and being dead tired, we immediately hit the sack. The next day, October 30th we set sail from New York Harbor to join a convoy with destroyer escort several miles out to sea. We spent eleven days crossing, and a very unpleasant crossing it was for most of us. The ship was crowded and ill fit for so many men, and the man who didn't get seasick was rare indeed...We occupied our time with card playing, language classes, calisthentics [sic], reading, inspections and deck-walking. It was on the 10th of November that the joyous sight of land, in the form of England and the port of Avonmouth, greeted our eyes."

"Every day of these six weeks was filled with intensive training on the mechanism, laying and picking up of mines, with emphasis on German mines..."

"On March 4th [1945], just 2 days after it had been taken, we moved into the city of Trier [Germany]. This city had been quite thoroughly destroyed by bombing, but we managed to find comfortable billets, besides plenty of wine. Using Trier as a base for about 2 weeks, we did many jobs, including road repair, mine clearing, removing road blocks and hauling lumber and other materials. We also built and repaired bridges on the supply routes."

"On May 5th we went to Vecklabruck, Austria, and two days later we learned that Germany had surrendered unconditionally. Little celebrating was done on this occasion, but there was a great relaxing of tension for all of us......On the 22nd of May we moved to Strasswalchen, where we worked on roads, loaded lumber, and guarded prisoners......On June 9th the company moved to Altenmarkt, where it still is at this writing. The present duties are guarding prisoners and loading lumber......"

Guarding prisoners was evidently a very important part of my father's experience serving in the army during his time overseas—but more about this later. My dad never talked much about his time in the service, but that was evidently quite common for those who had served in war time. He had said that both trips by ship across the Atlantic Ocean were long and uncomfortable, but the one home wasn't nearly as awful as the one to Europe.

His construction skills helped him get a job with the state highway department a few years after his return to the United States. Immediately after his discharge he bounced around from job to job for a while, from what I can surmise. But once he was employed with the state highway department, he stuck with it for many years.

His sense of humor served him well his entire life. He evidently had been tapped to serve as Master of Ceremonies for a variety show that he and his fellow G.I.s put on for other soldiers while they were all stationed in Germany after the war was over and the military helped with the reconstruction of that country. His old army yearbook had a photo of my dad, wearing *lederhosen* and a funny hat, standing at the microphone next to a captain (possibly his commanding officer). While a frequent teller of funny stories and jokes, my dad never seemed to be outgoing enough to be a Master of Ceremonies of any event. Seeing him in this role seemed strange to both Eric and me.

I brought Eric home to meet my folks just a few weeks after we started dating, as we got quite serious pretty quickly. Eric met my parents when Daddy was sixty-nine years old, and Ma was sixty-five. My father was just a couple of years older than Eric's mom. And my mother Rose was just a couple of years younger than Eric's father. While Eric's parents were quite vocal during their disagreements, my parents rarely argued and almost never in front of me. Eric felt that his father-in-law was "kind of a slug" in that he was not terribly motivated when it came to his career, and he was rather quiet and usually didn't have much to say. Lawrence had two speeds – slow and slower. He walked slowly, talked slowly, ate slowly, and so on.

My dad was good at woodworking and fixing small engine machinery like chainsaws and lawnmowers. Neighbors would come to him to get a picnic table or Adirondack chair built or to tune up their snow blower, etc. But it was almost impossible to pin Lawrence down for an exact date when he would have his work finished. He took his time and made sure it was done correctly, but not necessarily always within the customer's timeframe, especially if he ran into a glitch in working on the project. His attitude toward work was never overly ambitious, so he was not one of those fathers who spent all of his time at the office and none of his weekends at home. He was just the opposite. He was a family man, a homebody, and definitely not a ladies' man. His brother Harold was more the ladies' man, and would be the one to flirt with the pretty young waitresses when we all would go out to lunch, not my dad.

Lawrence had a desire to serve his community. He had certainly shown that when he enlisted to serve in World War II. In the 1970s he ran for Carterville's cemetery committee and was elected. In the early 1980s he campaigned to be a representative in the state's legislature. He served two terms before deciding that even local politics was too cut-throat for his taste. In early fall 1987, he decided that there should be a monument in the Carterville town center that was dedicated to the town's veterans of all wars. He put out a call to anyone in town who was interested in working on this project with him, and the initial meeting was scheduled for Veteran's Day. A couple of folks showed up, enough to get the project going, and an application for funding was submitted to the community fund. Other veterans in town joined the group to provide input, and the money was approved by the funding committee. On Memorial Day 1988 the monument was dedicated, much to my father's quiet pleasure.

In early June of 1994 my dad was diagnosed with terminal cancer of the esophagus, after months of noticing some difficulty swallowing. Just a few weeks earlier my mother had experienced a severe heart attack; we almost lost her a couple of times. That year was a terrible one for our family, as in addition to the serious health issues my parents were experiencing, Eric lost his job at the shipyard that summer as well.

With my dad's cancer diagnosis, and my mother slowly recuperating from her heart attack and regaining some strength very gradually, my dad knew he needed to trade in his beloved pick-up truck for a small easy-to-drive car. As his physical abilities declined, he knew my mother would need to take on the driving responsibilities once her strength improved. Seeing both of them decline in the same year was hard for all four of us. My dad underwent chemotherapy and radiation for a few months, which was awful for him. But this treatment seemed to temporarily halt the growth of the tumor. His health was stable throughout 1995 and even into early 1996. He was actually able to drive the two of them to my March 1996 graduation ceremony when I received my Master's degree. That was the last time that my parents, my in-laws, and my husband and I were all able to have a celebratory meal together.

A few months later he required hospice care and lost more and more weight. With the exception of a couple of particularly stormy days during the winter, my mother drove to the Hospice House every day to spend time with him. By April 1997 he was in his last few weeks of life, but his mind was still clear. When the Carterville minister visited him on the day of my parents' fifty-seventh wedding anniversary, he gave the minister the cash he had in his wallet and asked him if he would please stop at a florist to get some red roses and bring them to my mother on his way home. My mother had already had her daily visit with him earlier, and she was quite surprised when the minister came to her door with a beautiful bouquet of roses. We all appreciated this assistance very much. Daddy passed away a week later, with my mother and I in the room. It was one of the hardest days of my life.

CHAPTER 4

The Bombshell

Samuel didn't waste much time in responding to my email, taking into consideration the time difference between our locations.

RE: Research. I need your help

Hello Samuel,
   What is your research?
   My father was Lawrence Rollins, now deceased.
                                    Martha (Rollins) Levallee

The next day, I received my second email from Samuel:

April 10, 2014

Hello Mrs. Levallee,
   thank you so much for answering! At first, i must excuse myself if my english is not that good, but i hope you will understand me.
   I found your name after a long research, i am looking for someone who could know Lawrence Rollins for years now. The only thing i got is an address: Rollins, Lawrence. Carterville P.O. ME Box 14. The internet getting bigger and bigger, filled with more informations helped

me now to find your name. Anyway, i am not sure if your father is the Lawrence Rollins i am looking for. I want to tell you the reason for my research. Even if it's confusing....i don't want anything bad. To be honest, i am looking for my Grandfather. ....

At this point I just stopped reading. I could feel my anger bubble up quickly inside of me and my stomach twisted into a knot. My breathing became deeper and more forceful, and I had a hard time focusing on anything while my mind raced, thoughts tumbling over one another. When I read that he was searching for his grandfather, and implying that my father was his grandfather, I became boiling mad. I was just furious. How could this stranger even suggest that my father had cheated on my mother? Daddy would have never cheated on Ma. He was a good and honorable man. He loved her... they loved each other, and me, very much. He never would have done such a terrible thing.

I closed the email and tried to go about my work and put this stranger's insinuations out of my mind. But I had difficulty focusing on the tasks for my job. Eventually, after an hour or so, I had to re-open the email and read the rest of it.

.... i don't want anything bad. To be honest, i am looking for my Grandfather. My dad never did this, maybe he thought there would be never a chance to get in contact to his father. I feel like i am the only one who really tries to find out who he was and if there are relatives. It feels like one part of my family has always be lost. So i need your help. And ask you the important question if your Father has been (garrison?)...i mean was an soldier of the US Army and was in Berlin, Germany around 1945?

You are the only trace i got. So if you think we write about the same Lawrence Rollins please let me know. I can imagine that this all sounds weird and if your father really was this soldier maybe you never heard about this story please remember, i really dont want anything bad. I am just looking for my roots.

I hope to get an answer from you.

Yours, Samuel

I still felt livid reading this. I thought to myself, *This must be some scam artist who has come across the World War II Memorial's website, and he's picking names of deceased WWII vets and contacting their descendants to stir up trouble, look for money, or whatever. There is no way that what he is writing has any truth to it – it couldn't.* I tried to put this ridiculous claim out of my head for the rest of the day and focus on my work. Thankfully, I had some student email questions to deal with for the next few hours.

I got home that evening and showed my husband the email, and he could see that I was still fuming about it. Usually, Eric tends to be the one to fly off the handle quickly and I'm the more calm and slow to anger one. But not this time. Eric had to calm me down. He said to me, "Now let's look at this email message again. This young man sounds genuine – the language doesn't sound like he's looking for something or trying to con you. Maybe this young man genuinely believes that his grandfather's name is Lawrence Rollins – although we both know that just couldn't be true, knowing your dad."

I listened as Eric continued to talk me down from my anger.

"We know from your father's army yearbook that he was an emcee at a variety show for other G.I.s – even though it seems kind of hard for us to believe. But we've got the picture in that yearbook of him on the stage, with the microphone in the stand in front of him, while he was wearing *lederhosen* and other German-style clothing. So maybe one of the G.I.s in the audience was going to meet up with some little Fräulein that night after the show, and he didn't want to give her his real name, and so he grabbed the emcee's name off the program and told her that his name was Lawrence Rollins. That way he wasn't found out, probably being married or something."

I started to relax a bit, as this sounded plausible. And my father likely wouldn't have had any knowledge about it. So perhaps this young German man honestly believed that his unknown American soldier grandfather was named Lawrence Rollins, and he just wanted to know more about him, as he indicated in the email.

Over the next several days, my anger started to subside as I pondered this theory that Eric had proposed. I was still pretty upset about this whole situation though, and I emailed my best girlfriend and former college roommate, Sally.

Hi - Out of the blue, I got an e-mail (read from the bottom up) - I don't believe it but still, until I can look through the documents from my folks, it's unsettling to say the least.

Martha

My friend Sally wrote back:

Wow - I can see how unsettling this could be. If you continue contact with him. just be careful. I would probably keep doing it only from work. Big hugs ... Are you planning to look at your father's war records or let it go? Call me if you need to talk - if you get my voice mail I will call you back :)

Love -
Sally

Nearly a week passed, and I was in the process of starting to write a cordial email response back to Samuel; it had taken me that long to be able to compose something civil and not sound too angry. But even before I had finished creating the response message, I received another email from Samuel.

April 16, 2014

Dear Mrs. Levallee,

did you receive my last mail? I was so excited to get an answer and i decided to give you more time but now i am not sure if you will write back. Am i right? Do we talk about the same person?

I am sorry for writing you all these things. Be sure i dont want anything bad. I am serious. Please, if you know anything give me an answer. I felt so close finding your emailadress, now i feel lost. Please.....write back.

You are the only chance i have.

Yours, Samuel

I finished writing my response email to Samuel to let him know that I did receive his last couple of emails. And his most recent email genuinely sounded distraught at the thought that I might not respond to him.

Dear Samuel,

I did receive your last e-mail, and I looked for documentation regarding where my father was during WWII.

What month(s) of 1945 do you believe he was in Berlin? And why do you think that?

What documentation do you have that would indicate you are related to Lawrence Rollins?

And what other information do you have to indicate that the Lawrence Rollins you seek is the same one as my father?

Rollins is a very common name in the U.S.

> *Martha Levallee*
> *Academic Advisor*
> *State College*

I was calmer, but still quite suspicious of and miffed at this stranger and his accusations about my father's supposed infidelity toward my mother.

April 16, 2014

Dear Mrs. Levallee,

thanks for your answer. And thank you for looking up in your documentation. I can imagine that it feels strange getting an email from somebody unknown who klaims that he might be a relative of you. Therefore more than ever thank you, that you did not delete my mail and look up in those documents you have. Regarding to your question what documentation indicate that i am related to the Lawrence Rollins who was your father- to be honest right now i dont have much hints. I now that there excists letters that he wrote to my grandma. She died when my dad was abou 17 years old. Its several years ago that i asked my dad for more information. The only thing he gave me was his name, and as i wrote you in my last mail: Carterville P.O. ME, Box 14. So where did i find especially you? The internet helped my to find information about lawrence rollins from carterville. On a website of a cemetery i found his name, his date of birth seemed to be realistic. I think it was a few month ago i read about Rose Rollins on another website, it was like an article after her death where i also found your name. You know, i dont have much information. Only the hope and my strong will to find out who my grandpa was and to give my dad answers about his dad i keep searching for every hint i can get. I dont have the Letters right here at home but my father- who lives in another city- has those letters somewhere. I didn't tell him about my trace and our emails. But i'm gonna see him on easter day and ask him for those letters. I hope to get more information than. Maybe i also can take a picture of them. to give you more information. I'm sorry that i dont can give you more right now. My dad was born on November [X], 1946. Supposing he was normally born after nine month, my grandma and Lawrence Rollins must have met around February 1946. I dont know how long they knew each other, i dont know how long he stayed in Berlin. But be sure that i try to find out as much as possible about that the next days.

I don't want to be hasty, but you said you looked for documentation about your father in WWII.

Did you find something that could support my assumption?

I wish you a nice day and hope to hear from you soon.

Yours, Samuel

This email message helped soften my anger a bit. The writer did sound genuine, and not just out for scamming money or stirring up trouble. But I was still very skeptical.

I didn't have much left from Daddy's army days. I did have his army yearbook, which I rarely looked at because the book had developed a moldy smell and whenever I held it and spent more than just a few minutes looking through it, my sinuses would start to bother me. It contained the most detailed information I had about his army battalion and their travels and experiences. I also had his old "Enlisted Record and Report of Separation" form, which indicated the duties he had performed, and his entrance and exit and training dates. Nothing indicated that Daddy had ever been in Berlin. This was another reason why I thought Samuel must be mistaken in his facts. I would let him know that none of what I had for documentation indicated any connection to Berlin. And because I was so sure that the Lawrence Rollins he wrote about could not be the same person as my dad, it would take an awful lot of proof to convince me that anything he wrote about was true. I wanted to make it as difficult as possible for this potential con artist to scam me.

April 17, 2014

Dear Samuel,

No I did not find anything to indicate that my father was ever in Berlin.

I would be very interested to see anything you could show me from those letters – the addressed envelope, the handwriting, and most especially the signature at the end of the letter. So I hope you will be able to obtain them from your father when you see him for Easter.

Martha Levallee

Nearly two weeks went by without any additional word from Samuel. I figured he had been backed into a corner to show me documentation, and he couldn't… because there was none.

But then Samuel wrote to me once again and this time he had attached photos of two portions of a letter written by Lawrence Rollins: the very beginning of the letter and part of the ending of the letter including the signature.

April 29, 2014

Hello Mrs. Levallee,

sorry for not writing you for a while but i needed some time to get more information from my Father.

Furthermore he brought me a copy of the letter Lawrence Rollins wrote to his mum.

I asked him to tell me more about the time my Grandma met Mr. Lawrence, unfurtenately he doesn't know a lot. But i have a very important information! My father was born in Berlin, but Lawrence

Rollins has never been there! In fact my Grandma met him in a city named Deggendorf in bavaria. I dind't now that so far. My Grandma was interned there. She was brought to Deggendorf from somewhere in Italy. I dont now if she met Lawrence Rollins already in Italy or only in Bavaria.

With this email i send you 2 extracts of the letter i have. Please give a assessment if this could be your dad.

I hope you had a nice Easter and really hope to hear from you as soon as possible.

Take care,
yours Samuel.

When I opened the first attachment, I saw the date on it was from 1951, long after Daddy was home from the war. And although the handwriting looked familiar, I couldn't immediately identify if it was Daddy's or not, just based on the handwritten date. But I definitely recognized the first sentence: "Am feeling fine and hope you are the same" or similar variations, was the standard way my dad always started every letter he wrote. In fact, it was a standing joke in our home because my mother told me how frustrated she'd get with reading Daddy's letters that he sent home to her from the war that basically only said that. "I wanted to know more," she emphatically said. But there was so much redacted from his letters that she could barely get anything more than that from them. The U.S. government opened all letters sent from servicemen home and blacked out anything that could possibly compromise the Allies' war efforts.

I knew from that sentence and the familiarity of the writing that most probably yes, Daddy had written this letter. And then I opened the second attachment, and I saw the signature. Daddy doodled his signature over and over again in his late adult years, and so I did readily recognize his signature. He had definitely written this letter. Although I found it strange that he signed it "love," as he was married to my mother long before 1951, and I had no idea who this "Gretchen" was.

Since I recognized his signature and his opening line of the letter, I knew that Samuel and I were both speaking about my dad. I forwarded this email to my personal email address at home. From there, I replied to Samuel and attached three photos of my father.

April 30, 2014

    Yes Samuel, the handwriting on that letter is my father's writing and signature.

    And he usually began writing any letter with "Am fine - hope you are" or words like that.

    So I believe your grandmother Gretchen knew my father Lawrence.

    But please forgive me, it's difficult for me to believe that my father would have had a child with another woman in 1946 when he married my mother before he went into the service. It's shocking to me to think that he could have cheated on my mother like that.

    What is your father's name? What was your grandmother's full name?

    Can you send me a picture of either of them?

    I'm assuming Lawrence knew about your father.

    Can you send me the rest of that letter so that I can read all that he said in it?

    I've attached 3 photos to this e-mail - my father is on the left with the hat (and his father is on the right with the hat) in the first photo from 1943. His mother is in front and his 3 sisters are included in the photo.

    In the next photo the little boy with the dark suit is my father Lawrence when he was about 10 I believe.

    The last photo I took of my parents in 1976.

    I hope you and your father enjoy these pictures.

    I'll probably use this e-mail address now since I know there really is a connection between you and my father.

    I look forward to hearing back from you.

                                           Sincerely,

                                           Martha

I had sent this email message from home, so that I could attach some photos to it. It was another Wednesday morning, and per my usual Wednesday schedule, I went in to the office later in the morning and worked later into the evening. And because Europe is six hours ahead of us, I knew that Samuel would be able to view my response and these photos before too many hours had to pass, because he usually wrote to me in the evening, and it would be evening there not too many hours after I sent that email. I got ready to go to work and wondered what my next communication from Samuel might hold.

We were short one staff person in the front office that day, so I had to cover for my colleague Lucy when she went to lunch. But it was very quiet in the office that day and the phones rarely rang. I couldn't help but think about Samuel and when I might hear back from him and what his response might say. My curiosity got the best of me, and I used a front office computer workstation to check my home email to see if Samuel had responded.

To my surprise, not only had an email from Samuel come in, but his response included the scanned attachment of the full letter from my dad to Gretchen, as well as the envelope the letter was mailed in, and a photograph of Samuel's father when he was around thirty years old, as well as a more recent photo of him.

April 30, 2014

Dear Martha,

i must confess that i am really speechless. You know i never believed that i could find anything about my grandfather. I cannot belive that i found the right trace. Reading your mail and looking on the pictures felt so unreal. I didn't tell my father about this so far. When i saw the picture of him as a boy, i didn't need to guess who is lawrence. I saw it. I knew it. This is so incredible.

I can imagine that this situation is really difficult for you. I thought about this from my firt email on. But i had to find it out. You know... this is a lost part of my Family and a lost part of me. I want to know who my grandfather was. I don't know anything about him.

My Fathers full name is Rolf Jonathan Graf. My Grandmothers name was Gretchen Graf.

Lawrence knew about my Father as you will see when you read the complete letter. And he wrote about his wife and that she hide the letter so i guess she also knew.

I dont have a picture of my grandma. I need to visit my dad to see his old pictures of her. What i have is an older picture of my dad, i guess it was taken when he was i dont know, about 30 years old? I need to ask him. And anotherone, taken in 2011 when me and him visited berlin and he showed me the streets where he grew up. Its not a pretty good one but i think for now its okay.

Thank you so much for your cadidness and your help.

I really hope to hear back from you soon, too.

Yours,

Samuel

Then I opened each of the attachments. I shouldn't have been doing this at work, but my curiosity was too strong – I had to know more details immediately. There was no way I could wait until I got home that evening – I felt that if I waited I would burst!

September 30, 1951

Dear Gretchen,

Am feeling fine and hope you are. I just found the letters you sent me. My wife hid them on me. But she is not with me now. So I am writing you too see if you will sent me a picture of the boy. And if you want me to sent him something write me and tell me what he needs. And I will sent it. Write soon if you can.

Love, Lawrence

When I read the entire letter, even though Daddy did not specifically state that he was speaking about his son, I knew that he cared about both Gretchen and her son... Then I opened the attachment of the old black-and-white photo of Samuel's father. This blond man was nice looking, and I first noticed his dark eyes and dark eyebrows, which did not look like my father. But as I took in this man's entire face, the lower half jumped out at me as resembling my dad. This man had Daddy's mouth and chin. And similar hair, and the same shape of his face and head, and the same ears... I was absolutely stunned. This man had a deeper cleft in the middle of his chin than Daddy did, but the mouth looked just exactly the same. And although I did not have Daddy's military photo with me there at work, I remembered quite well what he looked like in it. Comparing it with this photo now staring back at me from the computer screen—the resemblance was incredible. I felt like an explosion had gone off in my body and my adrenaline level shot through the roof! I could barely catch my breath. My father had a son! I have a half-brother! I was absolutely ecstatic to learn this news. When I saw this proof, my heart started to race and I was simply overwhelmed with excitement. I couldn't believe it. Growing up, I had longed for a sibling. And, suddenly, in my mid-50s, I was no longer an only child. My beloved dad had a son. And not only that, but he had a son who looked a lot like him.

The second photo Samuel had attached was even more telling than the first one. In this color photo taken just a few years ago, my brother was standing on a street outside a brick building, looking slightly down and standing with his arms folded in front of him. This sixty-something man had a lot more hair than Daddy ever had while I knew him, but the hairstyles were very similar. And so many times I had seen Daddy stand outside with his arms folded, looking down as he pondered something. The stance and physique of this man in the photo very closely resembled my own father's.

I forwarded Samuel's email to Eric and then immediately called him at home. He was not there, and I had to leave a message for him on the answering machine. I could barely catch my breath; I was so excited at this news. It was like I had just opened the most wonderful Christmas present as a child, only magnified ten-fold. In the voicemail message to Eric, I said that Samuel had just sent me an email with actual proof that I did have a brother. "You need to check your email because I just forwarded the email to you so you can see these incredible photos."

Eric called me back just a few minutes later and asked, "Are you OK?" I was so excited that I'm sure it was rather difficult to understand my exuberant, breathless message. I assured him that I was super excited but fine, and we'd talk more about all of this when I got home that evening. Just then, one of my students walked into the office and I had to quickly compose myself and act professionally.

Somehow, I was able to calmly answer the student's questions and she went on her way; just then Billie came back into the office. I couldn't contain my exuberance for another minute. I asked Billie if she had a second, and she said sure. I grabbed the printout of my father's letter that I had just been sent, and the two photos of my half-brother, and followed her into her office. I told her that I had *just* learned that I had a brother.

She looked at me strangely, and I said that I had received an email a few weeks ago from a young man in Germany.

She sat up straight and her eyes got wide as she said, "I remember that."

I explained to her what had happened since that first email— about how I had written back and forth with this stranger, and that he had just sent me proof that I had a brother— and I showed her the pictures. Unfortunately, I did not have photos in my office of my father to show her, nor did I own a smart phone. But I described to her how much the two men looked alike. Billie looked astonished as I cried and laughed and described how similar this man looked to my dad. It was going to be a challenge for me to think of my father as anyone else's father. But these photos were undeniable proof.

Just a few minutes later Lucy returned from her lunch break, and I sat with her by her desk. She could see by my face and my breathlessness that I was exuberant about something. I told her that I just had to tell her my fantastic news; I just couldn't help myself.

She saw the look on Billie's face, and then looked at me and said, "Oh, I'm afraid to hear." (I think she was worried that I had just been offered a great new job and was leaving my current position.)

But I told her I had just learned that I had a half-brother.

She calmly listened to my announcement and then asked, "Your mom or your dad?" and I said my dad. I then told her my story and she, too, was very happy for me, shedding a tear as I recounted my story to her. It was probably another hour before I had calmed down enough to try to go back to work. But I really wasn't able to get much work done that day, as I was just too over the moon excited.

When I finally calmed down a few hours later, I responded to Samuel's last email.

Hi Samuel,

I'm stunned. Thank you so much for sending me the entire letter and these photos.

I really appreciate it.

I guess I need a few days to process all of this.

I'm sure you'll be sharing info with your father soon about all of this, right?

Martha

CHAPTER 5

The Potential Clues

After receiving the proof that I did indeed have a half-brother, I was a bundle of mixed emotions for the next few weeks. I had a very hard time staying asleep at night. I kept searching my memory, trying to find any hint or possible clue that I had missed. Gradually, I started to remember bits and pieces of incidents that would have been clues for me, if I had had any sort of inkling of what had occurred in my father's past. It was like I kept stumbling across jigsaw puzzle pieces, but couldn't tell what pictures they might be a part of, or even if they went together.

I remembered being in my early teens on a Sunday morning while my mother was at church, and Daddy and I were at home. Daddy rarely went to church, and although sometimes my mother dragged me along, those instances were pretty few and far between, thank goodness. I remember I was sitting in the living room, making out a family tree of the Rollins side of my family. I started with my grandparents, Albert and Edna Rollins, and I drew a tree that included their five children (Lucille, Harold, Lawrence, Gloria, and Darlene) and all of their grandchildren. To be sure that I hadn't forgotten anyone, I asked my father, "Daddy, Grandpa and Grammy Rollins had eleven grandchildren, right?" My father stared at me, his face blank and he thought for an extra moment or two. And then he quietly responded to my question, "They had twelve."

So naturally I thought I had missed one, and started my count again, going through each of the branches of the tree carefully. A few minutes later I replied, "Huh, I can only come up with eleven names," and he looked at me again and hesitated.

Then he asked me "Can you keep a secret?" As a young teenage girl, naturally I said yes. Then he said to me, with a twinkle in his eye, "One of the five kids had a child that nobody's supposed to know about."

I was very surprised and interested in this juicy gossip that was being presented to me. My response was, "Really?! Which one?" and of course he brushed it off.

He said that he couldn't tell me which one. I kept trying to push him to tell me and he wouldn't. In fact, he also said, "It would probably be better if you didn't mention this to your mother."

I looked at him, puzzled, and asked, "Why? Doesn't she know about this?"

And he said, "Well, yes she does."

That did not make any sense to me at all. Why shouldn't I mention anything to her when she was already aware of it? Never in a million years did it dawn on me that the "one of the five kids" to have a secret child might have been him.

Since I had always been very close with my mother, and told her pretty much everything at that time, I pounced on her as soon as she came home from church. "Ma! Guess what? Daddy said that one of the five kids had a child that nobody is supposed to know about."

She looked rather stunned at first, but then just brushed it off and told me, "Oh, we don't talk about that – just forget about it."

But this was just too juicy of a secret for me to "just forget about," and I continued to try to figure out which of my aunts (or possibly my uncle) it was. I immediately thought it must have been Aunt Darlene, the youngest of the five kids, because she had been married a couple of times, whereas all the other siblings had only been married once, each for many years. But then I remembered that the eldest, my Aunt Lucille, had gone to live with my grandfather Albert's sister and her husband in the state capital when she was a teenager, and graduated from high school in that city. Perhaps she had gotten pregnant as a teen and was shipped off to live with these relatives to have the baby and then put it up for adoption.

For the rest of that day, I wondered about this, and pondered it aloud to my parents. But that evening, my mother took me aside and sat me down to discuss this situation with me.

She looked me straight in the eyes very earnestly and asked me, "You have said before that Aunt Gloria is your favorite aunt, right?" and I told her yes. Then she spoke to me very slowly and deliberately, and her tone indicated she meant business. She continued, "Well, I'm *not* saying that it's Aunt Gloria, but I *am* saying that *if* you continue to ask questions about this, you will hurt someone *very* deeply – someone that you love just as much as – if not more than – Aunt Gloria."

The way she said it to me, I knew she was resolute about me leaving this subject alone. I remember wondering at that moment if she meant my cousins Tommy and Lucy, or their mother Leslie, or herself, or whom she possibly could be referencing, because there weren't many people that I could think of that I loved as much as – or more than – my Aunt Gloria.

I realized that I needed to just let this subject go. And I did, and surprisingly pretty much forgot about all of this. But the fact that Daddy had looked me in the eye all those years ago and told me that his parents had twelve grandchildren, including one that "no one was supposed to know about," made me realize *now* that he *wanted* to tell me that I had a brother. But he must have promised my mother that he would never volunteer this information to me.

Over the years, there were other "hints" I could have picked up on, had I any clue about this secret. Like on my first day of my sophomore year in high school, I came home and chattered away over supper about my first day of school, as I often did. As usual, my mother listened to me but my father only half-listened and tuned out most of my chatter. But when I told them the names of all my teachers, Daddy's ears perked up when I said that my English teacher's name was Mrs. Deutsch. Suddenly he became interested in what I was saying. He stopped me and asked if he heard me correctly, that my English teacher's name this year was Mrs. Deutsch. I told him that I would have her for the fall but I might not have her for the whole year.

He seemed very focused on this information, and he said, "Deutsch, that means German."

I said I didn't know, it was not a familiar word for me.

He told me "I want you to ask her tomorrow if she speaks German."

I looked at him strangely, because this seemed like an unusual request, especially coming from him.

He said, "Ask her if she speaks German, and if she does, ask her if she would teach you German."

I chuckled and said that I doubted if she would be willing to do that even if she *was* able to speak German.

But my father was insistent, saying, "I think it's important that you learn German. Tell her I'll pay her to teach you German."

Now this *really* seemed out of character for Daddy. I knew that money was not available for unnecessary things in our family. I told him I would ask her, but French was the only foreign language that my small high school taught. So for me to eventually get into a good college, I would need to take French in my high school – they didn't offer German.

But Daddy was adamant – I needed to ask Mrs. Deutsch if she knew how to speak the German language. And the next day, I did. I waited until class had ended and nearly everyone had left. Then I approached her desk as she straightened her papers in preparation for her next group of English students. I said, "Mrs. Deutsch, my father wants me to ask you if you speak German. He said that your last name means German and he wants to know if you are able to speak German."

She laughed and said that while her last name, Deutsch, did mean German, she did not know the German language. I thanked her and felt relieved that I had done what my father had asked me to do— even though I was a bit embarrassed to ask my new teacher this question— and that it would not go any further; the negative response from my teacher immediately nipped that idea in the bud. I informed my dad at supper that night. It had seemed very unusual that Daddy would make an offer to pay my English teacher if she would teach me the German language. It was just so out of character for him.

Of course, now I know why he felt so strongly about this.

Thinking back, I remember my mother would always respond to strangers' questions about whether I had any siblings with the statement "She's our only child." This was of course true because I was my mother's only child, and thus the only child that Rose and Lawrence had together.

There were a few instances where I would notice that my father would watch a little boy and his dad together, on the street or in a restaurant, and my father seemed to look at them longingly. After noticing this a couple of times and seeing it once again when my mother was not around, I asked him, "Daddy, do you wish that I was a boy?" kind of afraid what the answer might be.

He looked at me with a shocked expression, and said "Oh no, no, not at all!" But I didn't entirely believe him, after seeing the look on his face as he observed little boys with their dads. It made me feel inferior, that despite his negative response, maybe he actually would have preferred that I had been a boy. I always wondered if I had disappointed him. Now, after this revelation, I gradually came to believe that he had not been disappointed in me, but he most likely was disappointed that he had been unable to share any part of his son's life.

When I was growing up, we would routinely watch comedy TV shows on our little black-and-white TV set in the living room. Daddy liked to watch *McHale's Navy* which was set in World War II, and he especially liked Tim Conway's character. He thought it was a very funny show. But when *Hogan's Heroes* would come on, the mood in our house would change. I didn't understand why, especially when both shows were comedies about WWII. But even as a child, I could tell that the atmosphere was different depending on which of these TV shows was playing in our living room. *McHale's Navy* was set in the South Pacific, and featured "the enemy" as the Japanese, which was no problem for either of my mother or my father. *Hogan's Heroes* was set in Germany, and often there were pretty, seductive German women characters included in a scene or two of these episodes. In such moments, the tension in the air could be cut with a knife; even as a child I could sense it but didn't know why.

In 1970 when my mother's father was dying of cancer, he liked to watch the new soap opera that had just started on ABC called *All My Children*. Gramma started to watch it with him, since he liked it so much. And when my mother would go to visit them she would end up watching it with them, occasionally. Gramp died in the fall of 1971 and unfortunately I don't have very many memories of him not being sick, as I was so young. After Gramp's passing, Gramma continued to watch the show, as did my mother. I think it helped them both feel closer to Gramp, at first.

At times, when I would be home from school sick or on a school vacation, I would watch *All My Children* with my mother. Eventually I was watching both *All My Children* and *General Hospital* on as regular a basis in the summers and other school vacations as I could.

I remember that my mother always had kind of a soft spot for the *All My Children* character Phoebe Tyler Wallingford. I always thought she was a meddling old biddy, too concerned with what other people thought and sticking her nose into other people's business too much. One day I asked my mother why she liked Phoebe. Her response was something along the lines of how Phoebe puts on an act but actually seemed rather insecure, afraid of losing her husband, Dr. Charles Tyler, to Mona, his secretary. Dr. Tyler and Mona were close, but both had too much integrity to have an affair, even though Charles had not been happy in his marriage to Phoebe for quite some time. My mother relating to bitchy Phoebe didn't make any sense to me at that time. Why would she feel that way? She had such empathy for a soap opera character who, to me, seemed so off-putting. But evidently there was something about that character that Ma related to in some way. To me, my mother had no reason to be insecure about her marriage. My parents showed affection and got along well, and just seemed to really love each other. Daddy would never cheat on Ma. Or so I thought.

Later as a teen, I watched *General Hospital* and there was one story line that involved Dr. Monica Quartermaine accepting the illegitimate son of her husband Dr. Alan Quartermaine and his mistress Susan Moore. Monica even accepted the boy into her home and as part of their family when Susan died. My mother was watching an episode about this storyline with me one day, and there was a scene where Monica was accepting toward this boy. My mother emphatically commented that it was just *not* realistic that *any* woman would so readily accept her husband's bastard child into her home. After this pronouncement, she quickly left the living room and went to the kitchen to start supper. I thought that was a rather strange reaction. It seemed to come out of the blue, without any connection to anything. I just chalked it up to another instance of my mother's menopausal mood swings.

So many of my old memories popped up in my mind like popcorn. We had moved into our newly constructed house on Mitchum Road in the mid-1960s, when I was four years old. Shortly afterward, I remember Daddy got a visit from one of his old army buddies. I got the impression that while Daddy was glad to see this old colleague, he was a bit antsy about him being with us. My mother served the men coffee and the adults chatted for a little bit, and then the men went outside with me while I played in the sand and made sandcastles, as there was no lawn yet around the new construction.

At one point, this visitor mentioned to my dad something about it being "strange to see you with… them."

I could tell from the tone of Daddy's voice that he really didn't want to talk about whatever subject the man had brought up, and they spoke in hushed tones for a little bit. Then I heard Daddy respond to a question from the man with "my wife knows, but she doesn't" as he gestured toward me.

I asked my father what they were talking about, and Daddy gave me some nonchalant answer, like "grown-up stuff." The man didn't stay much longer after that exchange.

In thinking back on this, it seems this man was indicating he was accustomed to seeing my dad with his German girlfriend, the two of them spending time together. This, along with the fact that Daddy wrote "Love" at the end of that 1951 letter to Gretchen, supports the assumption that their relationship was much more than just a casual affair.

I recall being about six or seven years old, watching my father get dressed up and putting on his Masonic pin to get ready to go to a meeting. I asked him what the Masons did at their meetings, and he said it was secret. I asked him if they told secrets and he said yes, sometimes. I asked him if he had told any secrets and he looked at me with a sly smile and said yes. I asked him if he could tell me the secret and his response was, "Well, then it wouldn't be a secret, would it?"

And I agreed with him. But this memory made me wonder if he had shared the information with his fellow Masons that while he was serving in the Army just after the end of the war, he had an illegitimate son with a woman in Germany.

My views of having an older brother were shaped by what I had seen on the '60s TV show *Leave It to Beaver*: a slightly older male sibling who would run interference for the younger sibling when the younger sibling had a problem. And the older brother would also be someone to talk with, hang out with, commiserate with about mutual concerns, and so on.

One day when my parents and I were eating at the dinner table, I asked about my mother's miscarriages and whether she had been far enough along to know the sex of the babies. She told me that the first one, yes, they knew it was a boy, but the second one, no.

My response was "Oh – that's too bad."

Daddy asked me if I would have liked to have had an older brother and I immediately said "Yes!"

He asked me why, and I thought for a bit and then said, "Well, he could have helped pave the way for me in school and keep older kids from picking on me."

My parents both chuckled at this response, and my mother said, "He would have been so much older than you that he wouldn't have been in school at the same time as you – he would have finished school by the time you started school."

This took a minute to sink in – for me to understand that if my parents *had* a baby boy when my mother first got pregnant, that he would have been that much older than me. What benefit would that have been to me? I still liked the idea of having an older brother but getting assistance from him with school issues would not have been possible. I finally responded, while looking at my father, "Well, at least we could have talked about you and the funny things you do."

And Daddy slowly replied, "Well... yes... I guess you could have done that..." his voice trailing off. Then he softly said "...if you spoke the same language." I looked at him strangely, thinking that was an odd comment to make, and my mother immediately changed the subject.

One summer, when I was about thirteen, my mother's mother was having a spat with one of her neighbors. My grandmother could be rather difficult, and she was quite judgmental. I don't recall what the disagreement focused on with her neighbor, but it got to the point where my mother felt she needed to step in and play peacemaker between the two. Gramp had usually been the one to smooth things over when Gramma caused friction with others, but he had passed away.

I remember one summer evening when Ma drove us the twenty minutes or so to Gramma's. I was to stay with Gramma at her house while Ma went to the neighbor's to discuss the situation. A while later, my mother returned and relayed to Gramma the resolution, and whatever it was that Gramma needed to do she wasn't thrilled with, but reluctantly agreed.

It was a warm night, and on the ride home to Carterville the car windows were open. My mother said to me, "I certainly hope that *you* never have to apologize to anyone for something I have done."

This puzzled me and I asked her, "Why would I have to apologize to anyone for something you had done?" She responded vaguely, "Well, you just never know, because I certainly didn't think that I would need to apologize to Gramma's neighbor."

I replied "Well, even if I *did* need to apologize someday to anyone for something you had done, whatever you did couldn't have been that bad."

And she quietly answered, "You'd be surprised."

I think she believed she had said it so softly with the wind blowing through the car windows that I didn't hear her, but I did. I asked her what she meant but she just brushed it off and changed the subject.

Much as it pains me to relate this next anecdote, I feel that it is very telling. One evening while my parents and I were watching the evening news, there was a segment about "deadbeat dads." I might have been college age at this time, or perhaps late high school. Anyway, at that point my views were very black-and-white, good vs. bad. After the news piece was over, Daddy asked me what I thought of what we had just heard. I told him (with my mother right there in the room) that I thought it was terrible that some fathers did not provide support to their children.

Daddy asked more follow-up questions, probably to gauge what my response might be if I ever learned of what he had done. He asked me, "What if the dad can't afford to provide for the child?"

My response was "that is no excuse"; if the man fathered a child, he has a responsibility to that child to financially support it. And if that means working overtime or taking an extra job in order to be able to afford to provide for the child, then that's what the father needs to do.

Daddy listened and then after a few moments asked me, "But what if the father doesn't know where the child and the child's mother are?"

That took me aback a bit, but after thinking for a few moments, I responded, "Well, I would think that the father could contact the police or some other authorities, to find out where the child is, in order to send money for the child."

Daddy quietly responded, "Well, yes, I guess the man could contact the authorities to try to find the child."

And with that, the questioning stopped. In fact, all conversation stopped. And for the next few days, the house was quiet, and Daddy seemed somber... to the point where I asked him, "Did I say something wrong, Daddy?"

And he quickly responded that no, I had not said anything wrong. But I could sense that the conversation we had after the news show had caused him to ponder something or other.

One summer when I was in college, I started working as a cashier at a local summer attraction. To afford completing my bachelor's degree, I needed to work full-time during the summers. There were two elderly women associated with the organization, Gretchen and Bernice, and on one of my first days of work I was introduced to each of them. When I told my parents about them at supper one evening, my father made a comment. "Gretchen – that's kind of a funny name, isn't it?"

My mother seemed to glare at him for that comment. My response to him was "Well, I guess so, but I think Bernice is an even funnier name."

His reply was that he had grown up with a girl in their neighborhood named Bernice who was about his age, so he was more used to the name Bernice than he was to the name Gretchen. The subject was then dropped.

During another college break, I noticed how much my mother "waited on" my father, similar to how Edith waited on her husband Archie Bunker in the television show *All in the Family*. I asked her why she did so much for him, when it seemed like he didn't do nearly as much for her regarding chores around the house and such. Her response was that he does something that she asked him to do, which is very important to her. Thinking back on this now, I believe she had insisted that he end all communication with his former girlfriend and their son.

Many years later, after Eric and I were married, and both of my mother's parents had passed away, my mother's only sibling, my Uncle Willie, and his wife had bought Gramp and Gramma's house and moved in, downsizing from their large old farmhouse. A few years later, after they had made a number of renovations, their backyard served as the setting for their eldest granddaughter's wedding. My mother was to play the organ for the ceremony and on the big day she drove down early to her parents' former house to practice. Daddy and Eric and I followed along later, closer to the starting time of the ceremony. Daddy was in a surprisingly good mood, considering that he was going to have to spend the day with his wife's side of the family. He always seemed somewhat uneasy around his in-laws.

We arrived and chatted a while with some of the family before the ceremony, and then Daddy went off on his own for a little bit and left Eric and I to socialize without him. Eric and I noticed him chatting with his brother-in-law, my Uncle Willie. Later, when it was time to sit down for the ceremony, Daddy came back to Eric and me, and his mood had turned sour. This was readily apparent when a young woman walked by who was noticeably pregnant, and Eric made the joking comment to my dad, "she looks like she swallowed a basketball," trying to get a chuckle out of his father-in-law and me.

Daddy gruffly responded, "Well I had nothing to do with it!"

His angry response shocked both Eric and me, and we looked at each other quizzically. What in the world had brought that on? For years, Eric and I wondered why that little joke had evoked such an unhappy response from my normally easygoing dad.

After we learned about my German family, Eric and I became convinced that while Daddy was chatting with Uncle Willie (who could be an instigator at times), my uncle must have made some dig toward my father about his infidelity. In our opinion, that must have been what had caused Daddy's mood to change so abruptly at that wedding, especially around the subject of a pregnant woman. The letter my father had written to his girlfriend, which Samuel had scanned and emailed to me, included the statements, "I just found the letters you sent me. My wife hid them on me. But she is not with me now." Therefore, if my mother moved back home to her parents' in 1951 (as I suspect), when Daddy's letter was written to Gretchen, then I feel certain that Gramma told her son Willie about the circumstances. Or perhaps my mother herself told her brother Willie what had caused her to move back in with their parents. But the scenario of Uncle Willie possibly commenting on my father's infidelity made sense to my husband and me.

This whole situation *must* have affected each of my parents and their relationship a great deal over many decades, although they hid it well.

CHAPTER 6

Being Good

My mother was a huge influence on my life. She was a stay-at-home mom during my childhood, and she was thrilled to finally be a mother after so many years of yearning for a child. My mother grew up in a religious family that was involved in their local church and had instilled in her how important it was to live a "good" life. She in turn passed on to me this emphasis on "being good" and "doing the right thing."

This was certainly beneficial to me, but it also caused me anxiety that I wasn't being "good enough." I never skipped school, and never even tried a cigarette, either tobacco or the marijuana kind. I didn't drink alcohol until I was in college, and never went to parties in high school. I was at home doing homework most evenings, and I always tried to do well in school. I was often teased by the other kids in school about being a "goody-two-shoes."

I remember one time complaining to my mother about my classmates teasing me and she replied that she could relate because kids used to tease her about the same thing.

She said, "In fact, some of the Rollins family used to tease me about that as well, when Lawrence and I were first married."

I asked her how she got them to stop, and that stopped her in her tracks. She casually said that she didn't remember. I *now* think the members of Daddy's family who initially teased Ma about being a "goody two-shoes" stopped doing that when she took Daddy back after his infidelity.

Because of my mother being so good, living a good life and being a good person, I always felt like I needed to try to live up to her. Had I known as a teenager that Daddy had cheated on Ma, and that (probably) Ma had insisted that Daddy give up his son, I wouldn't have felt as strong a need to "be good," knowing that neither of them had been as good as I had once thought.

Growing up as an only child in a very rural area of the northeast, I was lonely. There were very few children nearby for me to play with, and the two that lived within walking distance from our house were from a wealthier family, with a large home with a barn and horses. The boy was my age but we didn't have anything in common and barely spoke to each other even in class. The girl was a couple of years younger than I and she was crazy over horses, which I was rather afraid of. My father, knowing that we could not afford anything to do with horses, instilled in me the fear of them. He told me that horses can step on your foot and crush it, and sometimes when riding a horse, it can get spooked and throw the rider off, causing terrible injuries. I steered clear of horses, and the neighbor girl who owned them.

Sometimes I would have play dates with my cousins Tommy and Lucy, and we got along well. We even all volunteered together one summer at the local hospital, getting rides to and from the hospital and our homes from either their mother or my mother. But Tommy and Lucy were busy with their own interests as we grew older and we kind of drifted apart.

When I was quite young, I called my mother "Mummy," but as I grew older and felt that this was too babyish, I changed to calling her "Ma." The reason I chose to call her Ma was because my father and his brother and three sisters called their mother Ma, and as a child I always wished that I had brothers and sisters to play with. My parents tried to tell me that siblings often caused as much frustration as they did pleasure, but I didn't care. I was lonely. In reflecting back now, knowing how badly I wanted siblings, it would have been somewhat cruel for my parents to have told me that I *had* a brother, but we had no way of knowing where he was and that I would probably never be able to know him. Although I believe that my mother wanted to spare herself from the secret getting out, as much as to spare me from heartache, I believe that she felt keeping this secret was best for everyone involved… at least everyone on this side of the Atlantic.

I was always "Daddy's little girl." While my mother would correct my errors, be they in attempting to play piano, sew, cook, answer the phone in a professional manner, do homework, and so on, my father rarely did so. While part of it might have been he didn't think the corrections were that necessary, probably a larger part was that he did not know the correct answer himself. I was able to sense that my grandmother— his mother-in-law— wasn't thrilled with him, even from when I was very young, and thus I always held this against my grandmother. Anyone who didn't treat my father with as much respect as possible was not on my best side. I had never known what in the world she had held against my wonderful father, but after I learned the truth, I had to cut her some slack and not continue to hold her memory with as much disregard.

My mother called her mother regularly on the phone, if not daily, then every other day. As Gramma grew older and lived alone, my mother wanted to check on her well-being. During one of her calls with Gramma, I overheard my mother's side of the conversation when they were having a disagreement. My mother must have thought I was outdoors or couldn't hear her, or else she was just oblivious to my presence in the next room. I heard my mother say that no, she couldn't do that... "because she'd take his side... because I know my daughter!"

I made a noise or something to cause my mother to suddenly become aware of my presence nearby, and she quickly lowered her voice and changed the subject. I believe now that my grandmother was encouraging my mother to tell me about my father's infidelity. Gramma evidently thought that I would be furious with my father for his betrayal of his marriage vows to my mother. But my mother was absolutely correct – even now, many years later, after an initial anger with him, I realized that the important thing was meeting and getting to know my brother and his family members, who are now *my* family.

CHAPTER 7

A Flurry of Emails

After receiving Samuel's last email, I had to review the messages over and over to wrap my head around these new facts. The attachments to the email had provided the proof I needed in order to be convinced he was telling me the truth.

April 30, 2014

Hi Samuel,

I'm stunned. Thank you so much for sending me the entire letter and these photos.

I really appreciate it.

I guess I need a few days to process all of this.

I'm sure you'll be sharing info with your father soon about all of this, right?

Martha

May 1, 2014

Hello Martha. You're welcome. I'm goong to see my dad on saturday. It will be the first time he will see pictures of lawrence. Its a very strange situation for him, too. Till this day he never thought there was a chance to find out anything about his father.

Take the time you need. I can only imagine how this situation must be for you. I am so thankful for your honest way of communication.

Yours,
Samuel

Then I wrote to my girlfriend again to update her. I had enjoyed a lengthy phone conversation with her when I saw the proof that Samuel was telling me the truth – that I did in fact have a half-brother in Germany. She let me ramble on and on, with a few questions that popped into her head as I was relaying all of this information and still working on processing all of it. She was very happy for me, but she also encouraged me to be somewhat cautious.

Hi Sally -

I hope your concert went well.

I thought you might enjoy seeing what I found for info on Rolf, laid along-side a photo of my father (holding me @ 5 weeks).

The resemblance is uncanny!

Supposedly this weekend Samuel is sharing with his father the info he found (me and the photos I sent to him of Daddy).

So hopefully I'll know soon if there is hatred or indifference or interest on his part.

I told Samuel I needed a few days to process all of this.

So my plan at this moment is to meet with our lawyer on Wednesday morning to ask some questions (and hopefully be reassured there is no need to be concerned). And then I'll tell Samuel that I'm happy and excited to learn more about both of them.

I'm hoping that there will be interest, if not now then maybe soon.

But I'm kind of prepared for him to want nothing to do with me. Eric is trying to prepare me for that.

That's all for now.

Love,
Martha

Eric had encouraged me to speak with our lawyer about all of this, to make sure that legally and financially there was nothing that I needed to be aware of or cautious about. And our lawyer was able to confirm this for me, which eased my mind somewhat, with all that was circulating through it on a regular basis.

May 7, 2014 –

Dear Martha,

last Saturday i met my father. My brother and his wife also where there. I told them about my research and what i finally found out with your help. I showed them the pictures you sent me and they confirmed my impression, that Lawrence has similaritys with my father. Especially the Picture when he was a boy looks much like my father did. And the area around his mouth is pretty much my father. They were stunned.

I feel that this is a very special sotuation for my father, too. I'm not sure how he feels. He doesn't show. But i feel that he has to process this news.

We also talked about you and your situation. They all showed much respect and gratefulness for your help. We know that this situation is special for both sides- but we had the advantage that we knew that there has been someone from the States, even [though] no one ever thought that we could find out who he was.

I know that this is a very very difficult and confusing situation for you. I am sorry for that. But i hope that if you would have been in my situation you would have done the same. Follow every trace you can get. Try to find out who you are. Try to give my father answers he never got.

My father gave my some older pictures of him, also one with his mum. He wants me to send you some.

With this email i will send you two of my dad, and another one of me. Its not a good one but i guess now after so many mails you should know who you are writing with. Its me and my girlfriend at cologne airport last autumn.

I really hope that you are okay. For me its such a pleasure to write with you.

If you want to know anything- just ask. I will try to get as many answers i can get. Unfurtenately this is a topic my older family in berlin kept silent about. So even my father knows hardly about it.

Thank you so much. I really hope to hear from you. But take the time you need.

Yours, Samuel

And my response back to him, after getting the "all clear" from our lawyer:

May 7, 2014

Dear Samuel,

Thank you for the wonderful gift you have given me!

I am thrilled to learn of the existence of you and your father, and I'm excited at the possibility of getting to know both of you.

You did not mention how many siblings you have, or if you have children of your own.

But I would like to learn about all of the offspring of Lawrence Rollins.

And I am happy to provide you with any information I can.

Obviously you read and write English, so I assume you are also able to speak it. Is that correct?

How about your father? Does he read and write and speak English?

But I am jumping ahead too fast. While I want very much to get to know your father and you, perhaps your father has bad feelings towards Lawrence Rollins, and also towards me.

Maybe he wants nothing to do with me.

If that is the case, I would be disappointed but I would understand.

I never knew anything about this until you sent your e-mail messages to me.

My parents kept this secret from me.

However, in wracking my brain to remember any clues about this at all, I somehow remembered a conversation I had with my father when I was a teenager (that was quite a long time ago now!).

As you could see from the photos I sent, my father was one of 5 children, and they referred to themselves as 'the kids'.

One day, my mother was not home, and I was thinking about my Rollins relatives and trying to remember all of my first cousins and make a list of their names.

So I asked my father, "Grandpa and Grammy Rollins had 11 grandchildren, right?".

And I remember he looked at me with a twinkle in his eye and a slight smile on his face and said, "Can you keep a secret?". Of course I said yes, even though I really couldn't.

Then he said "One of the 5 kids had a child that nobody is supposed to know about.", and I tried to get him to tell me which one. He wouldn't, but I automatically jumped to the conclusion that it was the youngest child Darlene because she was married more times than the others. Stupidly (and because I was always very close with my mother) I told my mother about our conversation soon afterwards. She told me "We don't talk about that - so just forget about it.", and she let me believe it was my youngest aunt, Darlene.

So I truly believe that my mother prevented my father from telling me he had a son. And I'm convinced that if my mother had died before my father, then he would have shared this information with me after she was gone. But that is not how things worked out.

I've rambled on long enough here.

I'm anxious to know your father's reactions to all of this.

Perhaps he needs more time to sort through his feelings about all of this, as I did.

Again, thank you so much for reaching out to me and telling me about this.

At the end of April 1997, I lost my father to cancer. Now, at the end of April/early May of 2014, I feel like I now have a piece of him back again.

I look forward to our future communications.

Yours truly,
Martha

CHAPTER 8

A Whirlwind of Emotions

After I received Samuel's photos of his father, both recent and from decades ago, I could see the strong resemblance between his father, Rolf,
and my father, Lawrence, and it just sent my emotions into a tailspin! My
entire body was pumping with adrenaline, and while there were pockets
of relief that gradually grew from a few moments to a few minutes to a few
hours, it was many months before that adrenaline level dropped back to a
sustained normal level. I would try to sleep and my mind would race; I'd
wake up in the middle of the night and be unable to get back to sleep. I
would be at work and there would be a lull in my day, I would think about
the fact that I had a brother, and I would get very excited again. And the
fact that my nephew was interested in knowing all about Daddy, and that
I was the only one who could provide him with a reasonably complete
picture of his grandfather, made me feel quite special.

At this point, I was dying to book a flight to Germany, grab my pass-
port, and immediately go to meet my brother and his family. But I knew
that this was not feasible because of many factors.

I had responsibilities related to my job and couldn't just drop everything to fly to Europe for a week or more. And since I had never flown
outside of the United States, I really wasn't comfortable heading to a foreign country with a language that I did not speak. Samuel indicated that
my brother did not speak English. For me to drop everything and fly over
there only to sit and stare at my sibling without being able to communicate

with him just didn't make any sense. But I knew that I *had* to make plans to go and meet him, and his family, unless he was against it. Since my dad had basically abandoned Rolf and his mother, it was possible that Rolf had negative feelings toward Daddy, and possibly toward me. I needed to proceed cautiously.

Over the next days and weeks, I would have extreme highs and feel giddy, wanting to shout from the rooftops "I have a brother!" as well as periods of sadness and sometimes anger. Initially I felt very angry toward Daddy. How could he have cheated on Ma? She was patiently waiting at home, living with her parents while he was in the army. And he had an affair, one that produced a child. I felt sad for my mother. She had not only been cheated on by her husband, but she knew that she had not been able to give her husband a child at that point, having suffered a miscarriage, even though she very much wanted to become a mother. Yet another woman had been able to give him a son. This feeling of anger toward my dad lasted for about three weeks or so.

In my Thursday evening aerobics class there was a man who often worked out near my spot in the room whose name was also Lawrence. That first Thursday that I learned my father had a German son, I went to aerobics class needing to blow off some steam. But I couldn't bring myself to even look at the Lawrence standing next to me. This poor guy had absolutely nothing to do with my family, but the fact that he shared a name with my father made me transfer some of that anger at my dad toward this stranger with the same name. Normally I would sometimes chat with him and usually at least say hi, but not that first night that I had this new knowledge. The following week I still could not speak to Lawrence but I was able to glance at him. The third week I could look at him again and manage a brief "hello." By the fourth week I was able to put aside my anger at what Daddy had done, and go back to my usual cordial relationship with this fellow exerciser.

As those weeks passed, my anger about my father cheating on my mother started to subside. With that, I started to feel sad for my father, who was never able to see his baby son, or hold his baby son, or know his son growing up. To the best of my knowledge, there was no communication between my dad and the mother of his son during *my* lifetime.

But because his September 1951 letter to Gretchen indicated that he had just found multiple letters she had sent to him (intercepted and hidden by my mother) and he requested a picture of the boy, that would indicate he knew he had a son by that date, if not earlier. I will probably never know for sure if he was aware of Gretchen's pregnancy when he headed home to the States. She would have been about three months along in her pregnancy when he was discharged from the army on May 11, 1946. And he probably had at least ten days crossing the Atlantic by ship to come home (his army yearbook indicated it took eleven days for them to sail from New York harbor to England). My guess is that he *did* know when he left Europe that she was pregnant, but it is just a guess. What sorrow he must have had during his lifetime, thinking about his son and all that he had to miss.

And as I pondered this more and more, I started to feel anger toward my mother, for having prevented Daddy from communicating with his son, and for keeping this secret from me. I felt certain that, based on the words my father wrote to his girlfriend in September 1951, he and my mother split up for a while over this situation. And I was positive that when my parents did get back together, my mother must have said that a condition of reuniting was that he *had* to promise to never have anything to do with "those people" over there ever again. After I was born, I'm sure my mother must have insisted that I not be told about my brother. I felt that my mother's jealousy toward my father's German girlfriend, and the shame of his dalliance, was too much for my mother to bear. During the times that she did not have to think about the situation, she could pretend that they did not exist and try to forget all about "them." This was her way of coping. It took me another few weeks before this anger at my mother subsided as well.

By the time my anger was switching from my father to my mother, it was Memorial Day. When I went to the cemetery in Carterville to put flowers at their graves I spent a few minutes there, talking to them, even though I know it's just their physical remains that are under the earth in that spot; their spirits are with me at all times. I good-naturedly scolded each of them, him for having "been a naughty boy" while in Germany, and her for having prevented Daddy from knowing his son and me from knowing about my brother. Somehow, confronting them with my new-ly-learned information made me feel a bit better. There would be no actual confrontation because they could not speak back to me, but having expressed my feelings out loud to them, adult to adult, somehow helped me to cope.

CHAPTER 9

Next Steps

I was so filled with emotion over this new information that I was not getting enough sleep, my mind racing, thinking back to what clues I could remember. I decided to take advantage of my employer's mental health benefits and go see a counselor. I must admit that each time I felt comfortable enough with someone to share this story, I had the opportunity to relive the excitement all over again.

I was thrilled to have the chance to retell the story to those that I thought would listen. And naturally the counselor asked me lots of questions about my parents and this situation. Over the next couple of months I met with this counselor a half dozen times or more, and she identified a very important point. Perhaps my father's German girlfriend had helped him a great deal.

She said, "We don't know what he would have been like if he hadn't had her to turn to, if he would have even come back at all."

I hadn't thought of it that way before. I had been angry at Daddy for his infidelity, but none of us could know exactly what challenges he faced during and immediately after that war, while he was still in the army. Perhaps he wouldn't have been able to handle what he had seen over there had it not been for her.

When I shared my story with the Carterville historian years later, he told me, "As a military man, I can relate to your father being a long way from home for an extended period of time, under the hardship, turmoil, and stress of war. There is a fog of confusion and extreme loneliness for normal life back home, and the girl you left behind, wondering if you would ever make it back to the States alive. There were always local girls around the overseas military bases. Sometimes when two people connected it was just innocent compassion for another human being, either a hurting soldier or a hurting local girl, and fate put the two beside each other."

During my sessions with the counselor, I would usually end up in tears. I often skipped wearing makeup on those days. One of my counseling days happened to be the same day as the going away gathering at our office for Billie, who was leaving our organization to take a job elsewhere. My boss, the man in charge of our campus (as well as another couple of campus locations), came by for the event and he knew right away when he looked at me that I had been crying and that I wasn't wearing my usual makeup. Plus, my counseling session had lasted into the beginning of Billie's party, so when I arrived late, looking like I did, he knew something was up. It wasn't like me to be late for anything.

After the party ended, he came to my office to inquire if everything was alright with me. I motioned for him to come in and I got up and closed my door. Then I told him that I had recently learned incredible news, and I was seeing a counselor to help me process it all. I told him my story, weeping; he started to cry, too. He was very moved by what both of my parents had gone through, and what I was dealing with now. I told him that I intended to go to Germany to meet my brother and his family. Because my nephew had told me that my brother did not speak English, I would need to learn some German to be able to have a conversation with him. It would be a little while, but I would need a couple of weeks off from work for that trip. He told me that he would support me one hundred percent in my effort to go meet my brother. It was a relief to hear him say he would go to bat for me when I wanted time off for this important trip.

Up until this point, Samuel and I had pretty much been simply hitting "reply" to respond to each email that we received. I sent Samuel a warning about the potential for computer viruses to attach to our one long back and forth email thread. Samuel responded with a new email thread with many delightful details about his family… who were now becoming my family as well.

May 10th, 2014

Dear Martha,

thanks for the warning. I'm not a computer expect, too but i think your right. We shouldnt always just click on the answer-button. But were you able to save the pictures i sent you?

So i try to answer the questions i didn't answer in my last mail.

I have three siblings. An older sister and brother (38 and 34 years) and a younger half-sister (22). These all are children of my father Rolf. But i am much more closer with my older siblings. My parents got divorced when i was about 2 years old. My father told me, that he sent a picture of him, my mum and my siblings to the Address he got from the letter around 1986. But i told him that i assume the address is only a post box so nobody reached the letter.

I read, write and speak english (i try my best). My father barely speaks english. When he brought me the letter of Lawrence he asked my to translate it. But i am glad that i can help him. My siblings speak english, but not as good as i do.

I was really amazed about the conversation you had with your father many years ago. It makes me a bit sad to read that he died in 1997- my father and Lawrence could have had so many years together (if they lived on the same continent and the knew each other)

As i wrote in my last mail i am not sure about my fathers reactions. He is not angry at all. neither on his father or you! How could he be angry with you? I think that one reason he has no idea about his father is that my grandmother never wanted him to ask about his father. I guess she was emancipated and too haughty to ask for help and wanted to educate his son on her own. Lawrence asked in his letter if she needs anything. Berlin after WWII was totally destroyed and i believe that she needed a lot but wouldn't have ever asked for it. I think my father still needs some time but is interested. He asked about you, what is your job, what you look like and things like this. I think that he has to process a bit the fact that from one day to the other there really is someone who knows Lawrence.

You said that Lawrence had 4 siblings. What about them? Are they still alive? Or do they have children? If so, did you told them about me? And what about you? I read that you are married. Do you have children on your own?

I felt really stirred reading the things you wrote about your dad and that it feels like having a piece back again. For me it's so incredible. I am so speechless that i found you. It feels unreal. And i am so thankful about your reactions. That you don't judge me or are denying because now you know that there is a son/brother in germany.

I am sorry that i usually need some days to answer. But i have to concentrate a little to write in english and have to take some time to sit down and write.

I hope everything is fine and hope to hear from you again soon. Telling a good friend of mine about our mails i told him that you are an aunt virtual. This sounds a bit weird but i guess thats what you are. "Half-" at least.

I still have so many questions but i think thats enough for today.

Yours Samuel

May 10th, 2014

Dear Samuel,

Thank you so much for your response. I will sleep better now that I know Rolf does not have any ill will towards our father or towards me.

And thank you for explaining why it sometimes may take you several days to respond to my messages, and I completely understand.

I so appreciate your thorough descriptions and your honesty as well.

And you do VERY WELL with your English - I understand exactly what you are trying to say.

I, on the other hand, do not speak any German. So I guess I'm going to have to learn some!

Part of me wants to start planning a trip to Germany to meet you all (or as many of you as possible).

But 1.) I don't want to scare you off, especially not Rolf when he may need quite a bit of time to get used to this new information - his sister!

And 2.) I feel like I should learn some basics of your language before I go there.

I hope you don't think I'm being too forward in saying that I hope to meet you all some day soon. What are the names of your brother and sisters?

Perhaps a step before traveling might be for us to try Skype. I used this free software when I was taking online courses for my PhD program.

Perhaps you are already familiar with it.

Yes, I was able to save the latest photos you sent to me. Thank you - Lawrence would be so pleased to see he has such a handsome grandson!

Attached is a 20-year-old photo of my mother, my husband Eric, and my dad and me. As you can see, I look much more like my mother than I do my father. This was one of the last photos of my father before he was diagnosed with cancer.

I too feel very sad that my father and his son never had the chance to know each other.

Eric worked for several years at the U.S. Postal Service, and he feels quite certain that if Rolf mailed a letter and photo, addressed to Lawrence Rollins in Carterville in 1986, then most likely if that letter did not get returned to Rolf, then it made it to my parents' home. Carterville has always been a very small town, and I would guess that the Carterville Post Master would have known how to get it to him. But even then, when I was an adult, they could have told me about Rolf. I wish they had.

Eric and I have been married almost 26 years, but we never had children. Part of why I am so excited to learn about all of you is that I don't have much family left (in the U.S.). Every one of the people in the photos I sent to you previously is now dead. And I think I mentioned that Grandpa and Grammy Rollins had 5 children and 12 grandchildren (including Rolf). Of those 12 grands, only 7 of us are still alive. Of those 7, I am the youngest, and just today I called Donald (the oldest) and told him of you all. He told me that when he was a young man, just back from serving in the military, he became quite close with his Uncle Lawrence, and picked up on his hints about his girlfriend overseas. So he wasn't totally shocked to learn about your father's existence, but he said he had not known any specifics. I attach a photo of Donald and his wife and a daughter here; I think there is a bit of resemblance between Donald and Rolf. Donald is the eldest son of Harold, Lawrence's brother.

Eric and I went to the Daytona 500 race in February 2012, and the day before the race, we spent time with Donald and his family who live in Florida, about an hour's drive North of the Daytona Speedway. Eric is a big fan of NASCAR auto racing and usually when we travel, it's to a race.

I have accepted your Facebook friend request, and you'll be able to see more recent photos of me on my Facebook page. You'll see from one of my prominent photos that my husband Eric and I were able to meet Steven Tyler and Joe Perry from the rock group Aerosmith at one of their concerts. This was almost 7 years ago now. I see from their fan club web site that they, my favorite rock group, are playing in Dortmund on June 18. Have you heard of them? They are very popular here in the U.S. and they have done world tours. But I don't know how popular they really are outside of the U.S.

But I digress.

I work as an academic advisor at a college 'for adults'. Most of our students are in their 20's and 30's, needing more college education to progress in their careers. Classes are evenings or online. It is State College and is a smaller sister institution to the University. I have been there almost 12 years now. Is your father retired or still working? Eric retired a couple of years ago and loves it.

I do plan to tell other cousins about you all. But I honestly don't see them very often, so it will probably be a gradual process.

I completely understand why you wanted to know about your heritage, and your father's relatives. I am so thankful that you were successful in finding me! In a few days I plan to put flowers at the graves of both my parents and Lawrence's parents. Since he passed away, I have put flowers on his parents' grave every spring because he always did so, and I feel he would want me to continue this since he cannot. The grave plots are next to each other, in Carterville. If you'd like, I will try to remember to take a couple of photos while there and send them to you.

I have written quite a bit, and it must be tiring for you to read/translate all of this.

Take your time.

I look forward to our next email exchange.

Your Aunt,
Martha

May 10th, 2014

Hi Samuel,

Just a quick note here - I forgot to ask what your siblings names are!

Oh, and if you think it would hurt your father's feelings to tell him that I believe his letter DID make it to its proper destination in 1986, then by all means, don't tell him. The same goes for anything I tell you (or send you, such as photographs) - if you believe it is better for Rolf not to see/know certain things that I share, then trust your own judgement. I certainly don't mean to hurt anyone's feelings.

The attached is an example. It's a photo of my father holding me when I was 5 weeks old, pasted on a printout of information I found on the internet about Rolf. Perhaps Rolf would not want to see Lawrence holding me as a baby, when our father never got to hold his son. :-(

But as you can see, the resemblance is uncanny!

Yours -
Martha

I kept my girlfriend Sally updated regularly regarding this situation, usually by emails.

May 12, 2014 –

Hi there-

How did things go w the lawyer? No worries I hope!

Sally

Hi Sally,

Great! No worries - although he's a good lawyer and suggested that we have our trust paperwork updated to remove all references to both my mother and Eric's Dad since they are both now deceased. While there's little chance, I'm sure, that my lawyer brother would be looking for any financial gain from ME (of all people!), our attorney felt it a safe move (based on Eric's relatives also) to 'make it cleaner' and get rid of any references to our parents in our documents.

I now know that I not only have a brother and "a" nephew, but I have 2 nephews and 2 nieces!! Rolf was married to his first wife and had a daughter and 2 sons, Samuel being the youngest; and then he divorced their mother and, with another woman, had a daughter (who is now 22). I don't know their names yet. I still find it incredible that Lawrence Rollins has 4 grandchildren!!

I also telephoned my eldest cousin Donald Rollins in FL on Saturday, and after some probing questions and releasing SOME of the info at first, he admitted that after he got back from being in the service he became closer with 'his Uncle Lawrence', and picked up on hints he gave that there was a girlfriend overseas during WWII. Donald never knew there was a child, but he was not surprised to hear that I had learned of Daddy's infidelity to my mother. But Donald was very nonchalant about the whole thing and encouraged me to go to Germany to meet my family.

Oh, and this weekend I placed an order for Rosetta Stone to learn German! I'm sure Eric will pick this up much better than I, as he's already fluent in 2 languages and he watches a lot of documentaries about WWII so he hears snippets of Germans speaking their language (from decades ago, yes, but he's experienced that quite a bit over the last few years).

Got to go now - thanks for checking in!

Love,
Martha

May 14, 2014 –

Dear Martha,

i am sorry it took some time again for me to answer.

I didn't talk to my father so far. I don't see him very often, even he lives in the city next to mine. 3 years ago i moved out to live in cologne during my time at university. since last september i live in an own small flat. I was so happy to hear of your plans making a trip to Germany someday. Dont be scared of the language. Most Germans speak some english, especially in bigger cities. You know my girlfriends best friend, who is also a very good friend of mine went to boston a few month ago to work as an au pair. We thought about visiting her around new years day. Boston is not that far away am i right? So this might be an opportunety for us to meet in the US. I know skype, didnt't use it for a while now but i agree that this would be a nice idea to talk. Its still incredible to see Lawrence on pictures. I never met this person but i know that this is my granddad and he is the origin of me and my siblings. They are named Erik and Christina. I will send you a picture of last Christmas. The little girl at the roof is my sisters daughter Sonja. She is 2 years old. The woman on the picture is my mum.

What type of cancer did Lawrence have? You know this might be interesting for my family, maybe for some precaution. Especially because also my fathers mum died of cancer.

:-) Aerosmith is famous all over the world i guess! So of course, i know them! Dortmund is pretty close to Cologne, like an hour drive.

Yes, if you are at your fathers grave someday, i'd love to see some pictures. And i definetely want to visit this place someday!

My girlfriend Marla is about to visit me in an hour and i promised her to cook some food. So i will start working in the kitchen now. We both live vegetarian. She much longer than me. Passing on meat showed me some very good new stuff and i love to cook!

By the way i was in the US twice. When i was 15 i made a three week exchange programm with my school to Cleveland and in 2008 i visited my host family again. When i was there i often thought about

Lawrence and talked with the american family about it. I never
thought that i would find him.

 I am so glad i found you!

Take care,
Samuel

In reading his email again thoroughly, I noticed that Samuel indicated his brother's name was Erik, almost the same as my husband's name, Eric. My family now included two men, one American (my husband) and one German (my eldest nephew), with identical sounding names.

When I read that Samuel and his girlfriend were seriously considering coming to Boston to visit her friend for New Year's Eve, I was ecstatic! I was thrilled at the prospect of meeting my nephew.

CHAPTER 10

More Realizations

When I saw the photo taken at Christmastime of Samuel and his brother, sister, and mother, I stared for a long time at their mother. This woman looked vaguely familiar. From Samuel's email, I knew that my brother had sent a letter and photo to Lawrence in the mid-1980s. (Samuel had previously written: *My father told me, that he sent a picture of him, my mum and my siblings to the Address he got from the letter around 1986. But i told him that i assume the address is only a post box so nobody reached the letter.*) Seeing Samuel's mother in this photo reminded me of a long-forgotten event.

I moved to my own apartment in 1985 and I did not meet Eric until 1987, and in between I often visited my folks on weekends. I remember visiting my parents one day and seeing an envelope with overseas postmarks/stamps on the small table between their chairs in the living room. I was alone in the room, as my mother was working in the kitchen and my dad was out in his workshop. At first, I thought it was a letter from my mother's longtime pen pal from France, Simone. To my knowledge, the only foreign mail arriving in our house was from Simone, and in that moment I misread the envelope as saying "Mrs. Lawrence Rollins," but it actually was addressed to "Mr. Lawrence Rollins." Since the envelope was opened, I peeked inside at the contents and saw a photo and a handwritten letter, which was common for mail from Simone.

My mom always let me read her letters from Simone. In fact, when I was in high school and taking French, she encouraged me to read anything written in French (including the back of any photos) to see if I could interpret what had been written. My mom hadn't used her French since high school when she and Simone first became pen pals. So as an adult she was very rusty, and many times she needed her French/English dictionary to try to translate the words. And Simone's handwriting had deteriorated over the years, so it became particularly challenging to decipher what she was attempting to communicate. Between trying to read what words were being written and then looking up those French words to then translate the messages into English was unquestionably a challenge. My mother usually welcomed my help with this once I became a young adult.

But this letter's salutation was "Dear Lawrence," whereas I expected it to say, "Dear Rose," as Simone's letters usually did. And although both this handwriting and Simone's were difficult to read, they were different. This writer was obviously not as proficient at English as Simone. I tried to understand what the writer of this letter was saying. I read through it a couple of times and looked at the photograph of a tall slender blond man, his slender but shorter wife, a young girl about ten years old, and a little boy about six. None of these people looked at all familiar to me. After reading it several times, it almost sounded like the writer somehow thought that Lawrence was his father, but the poor-quality English made me question my interpretation. Then I noticed the signature at the end of the letter appeared to say "Rolf."

I probably should have just put the letter and photo back into the envelope once I realized that it was *not* from Simone, but I was curious. And the envelope was right out in plain sight. I assumed that anything left out on the table in the living room was not terribly secret. I called out to my mother in the next room and asked her what this letter was, who it was from, and who was in the photo.

A few seconds of silence followed and then my mother came into the living room *irate*. "How *dare* you look into our personal private mail?" she bellowed.

I told her that it was just lying there on the table, out in the open, and because of the overseas stamps and postmark, I thought it was from Simone. I said, "You always tell me that it's fine for me to look at your letters from Simone, and that's who I thought it was from."

She continued to rant and rave at me about looking at the letter, and her strong reaction seemed very strange to me. Even though I had seen her fly off the handle at little things during her years of menopause, at this point that was quite a while ago. Her anger seemed out of proportion to my action. I apologized, but again asked my question of who was this man who wrote the letter? It almost sounded like he thought for some reason that my dad was his father.

She told me, "He's just confused – he's the son of a guy your father knew in the army and he's very confused. Just forget it!" She stormed back into the kitchen, and I decided that maybe I should leave and let her cool down.

I went out to Daddy's workshop and told him what had happened. I explained that I had seen an opened letter and photo in an envelope with foreign postmark and stamps and assumed it was from Simone and looked at it, and when I asked Ma about it, she got really angry with me.

Daddy asked me, "What did she say about it?"

I replied, "She said it was written to you by the son of a guy you knew in the service, and that this son is very confused."

After that, it seemed like my dad was even more quiet than usual. I then told him that I thought the man in the photograph looked a tiny bit like him, and he quickly looked up at me with what appeared to be happy gratitude in his eyes and he replied, "You do?" But then he caught himself and changed his demeanor back to detached again as he quickly looked back down at his workbench and again went silent.

I told him that I thought it best if I let Ma calm down and I'd head back to my apartment. He agreed that was probably a good idea, and so I called out to my mother that I was heading home and I left.

At this point, I had completely forgotten about the conversation I had with Daddy over a decade before where he let me know that "One of the five kids had a child no one is supposed to know about." If that memory had been less buried, I might have asked my father more questions, even if it meant risking my mother's wrath. But in that moment, I let it go and didn't push it, to avoid further upsetting my mother.

In some of the photos that Samuel had recently shared with me Rolf looked a great deal like our dad, but in other photos it was difficult to see much resemblance at all. Back in 1986 in this particular photo, I did not notice that Rolf looked much like my father. But Rolf's wife in that photo looked exactly the same as in this newest photo Samuel had emailed to me of his mother and older siblings.

While I felt foolish that I had let this opportunity slip by, I was grateful that Rolf had reached out to our father, and that letter had made its way to Daddy several years before he became terminally ill. It must have been a relief to him to know that his son had turned out fine, with a good career and a wife, daughter, and son.

May 14, 2014

Dear Samuel,

I would love to meet you in Boston around New Year's.

That would be wonderful. You are right, Boston is not that far from here. It's too far to commute to work every day, in my opinion (although there are some people who live in this area who do that). But it's certainly not far to go to see anyone from my newly-found family.

I know you and your girlfriend would primarily be in Boston to spend time with her friend, but I would so enjoy meeting up with (all of) you.

Depending on how long you were staying and if you had the time, I'd be happy to show you around Carterville. Winter is not the best time to see it, but if you are interested (and there isn't a terrible snow or ice storm) I would be happy to show you some places of interest there. It's VERY small, and not much to see - lots of woods, ponds, fields, etc. But then at least you could say that you had been to your grandfather's hometown. Even if you only had time for Eric and I to meet you all in Boston for a meal, that would be fun.

When I saw the photo of your mother and your siblings, the sight of your mother looked familiar.

Samuel, you are not going to believe this.......

She looks about the same in this photo as she did in 1986 - am I right?

I think I saw that letter and photo of her, Rolf and your older siblings as children!

........*My mother told me that the letter was from the son of a guy Daddy knew in the army. I asked her why he was sending Daddy a picture and she said he was just confused and I should forget it.*

Now I feel so stupid!! I had the chance to learn more about your family almost 30 years ago and I let it go.

My mother was so adamant about it being nothing and I should forget it (and she had never lied to me before), that I did as she instructed.

I should have questioned my father more about her reaction.

Since it was so unusual for her to act that way, I shouldn't have brushed it aside.

You are probably getting a very bad impression of my mother. She was really a wonderful person. But she grew up in a very strict family, and they were very religious. And her younger brother Willie not only served in the military during WWII, but he was also a prisoner of war in a German POW camp for quite a few months. So this situation, being 'scandalous' for that time, was all just too much for her to bear, I'm sure. She might have wanted this secret kept because she couldn't deal with it. Or maybe she thought she was protecting me..... from whatever.

Anyway, if you and your girlfriend (and perhaps her friend) were able to come to our home for a meal, I could try some of the recipes in the vegetarian cookbook I bought a few months ago. So far I've only tried one, and it was pretty good. My husband is more of a 'meat and potatoes' kind of guy.

Yes, I'm very glad you found me too!

That's all for now.

Your Aunt,
Martha

P.S. I may not specifically say it each time, but I want you to know that I am so thankful for all the information (including pictures) you share with me.

If I had pushed my parents to tell me what was so emotionally charged for my mother about that letter and photo, or if I had put together all of the clues myself and figured their secret out at that time, how would our relationship have changed? Obviously, I cannot be certain. But I believe my relationship with my mother would have suffered. And perhaps that was what my mother feared the most, first the possibility of losing my dad to someone else, and then losing the close relationship she and I had.

May 16, 2014 –

Hi Samuel,

Today I created a diagram of your U.S. family (as much as I know). It's attached.

If you have questions about it, please feel free to ask me.

I have also attached some photos from my visit to the cemetery.

What do you and your siblings do for work/professions?

Does your father still work or is he retired?

Oh, I re-activated my Skype account. My name on it is Martha Levallee in case that helps you find me.

I looked for you and there were a couple of accounts with your name so I wasn't sure what to do next.

> *Take care -*
> *Martha*

Hi Again Samuel,

I'm interested to know if your grandmother ever married, if Rolf had a father figure in his life while growing up?

I'm sorry if I'm overwhelming you with e-mails right now.

I'm just so excited to share information with you!

> *Yours truly,*
> *Martha*

May 21, 2014 –

Dear Martha,

thanks for all those pictures you sent me. Especially the grave ones. My father is in berlin till next week, i hope to see him than and tell him about our mails and pictures. And show him the diagram! I talk-

ed with my mum about this topic. Even they are divorced they phone sometimes. But she told me that he dindt't tell her in any word about thi lawrence story. Of course my mum knows about my research . She expected him to say in a few words like "did you hear about Samuels research...?" but he didn't. So my mum told me that she thinks he has still to work on it. My father doesn't show many feelings. So i still can not say what he really feels.

No my grandmother never married. My father had no dad in his life. And when he was 17 his mother died.

As carterville seems to be very small i send you a picture (not made by myself) of cologne, the city i live! i life in the pretty middle of it, i walk less than 10 minutes to the grand cologne cathedral.

I studied social work (as my both parents did) and work at an ele-mantery school in a part of cologne with many deprived children. But my contract ends on july 31th so i am writing many applications right now. One of the reasons i do not answer you mails so fast.

With this mail another picture of my dad when he was i think 17. not sure if i already sent it to you.

maybe my webcam arrives the next days so if you want we could skype.

Take care
Samuel

May 22, 2014

Dear Samuel,

Thank you for your update. I hope you are able to find a new job very soon, and I completely understand if you need extra time to respond to me. Searching for a job is a lot of work, I know! This is especially true when you already have a job.

I really hope that you find something well suited to you, especially if that will help you be able to come to Boston at New Year's!

It makes me sad to know that my brother had no father figure in his life while growing up. And that his mum died when he was so young.

He is obviously a self-made man (I don't know if that translates well or not). I am very proud of him for accomplishing so much in his life. And you too have obviously decided to work towards helping children in need as well - what a wonderful vocation you have chosen!

To be honest, I am seeing a counselor to help me sort through all of my feelings about this situation. My counselor told me that probably Gretchen felt that she needed to shelter and protect her son from those who still considered Americans to be 'the enemy' shortly after World War II ended. Maybe that is why she did not want Rolf to ask many questions about his father. Perhaps she felt that the less he knew, the safer he would be. But this is just a guess on my part.

Thank you for sending me a picture of your beautiful city. I'm really looking forward to seeing it.

When you have some time to set up your new webcam and feel ready, I would be very happy to Skype with you. But don't feel rushed.

My Rosetta Stone - German language CD's arrived yesterday, so this weekend I will probably start trying to work on that a little bit.

I am in the middle of a 12-week course that I am taking for my job, so I won't have as much time to devote to learning German as I would like until after that course ends in late June. But so far, just from playing on the Google Translate web site, I'm practicing saying "Mein Bruder lebt in Deutschland". :-)

Good luck with your job search!

Yours -
Martha

May 25, 2014

Dear Martha,

this was a very good weekend. On Saturday my parents in Law celebratet there 25 year marriage. And today my Mum celebratet her Birthday with a lot of friends. I met my siblings and told them about our last mails. My sister told me that she thinks that our dad is glad that i found you but doens't know to handle this new situation yet. He is back from berlin since today, maybe i call him tomorrow. I have a

job interview on tuesday and am a bit excited. Celebrating this week-
end we had some good beer wich is made in cologne and not sold
in whole germany. its a pretty regional product. Why i tell you this?
Next month the world soccer championship starts in brasil. And to
this event thee brewery made special bottles, not with their usual label
but with labels of all the participants of the World Cup. Guess wich
bottle i chose?! :-)

Hope everything is good in the US, i will read a bit now for my
interview.

> *Take care,*
> *Yours Samuel*

I was very happy to learn that Samuel's sister (my niece) believed their father was pleased to learn of my existence. I hoped he was coming around to communicating with me, in whatever language.

It took me several weeks to wrap my head around the facts of my new family, so it made sense that he would need some time also.

May 28, 2014 –

Dear Samuel,

I hope your job interview went well.

Maybe your father will need more time to work things out, but

I wonder if any of your siblings might be interested in e-mailing with me?

I love messaging with you, but you shouldn't have to shoulder the whole burden.

It would be fun to connect with them as well, I bet.

Even if they can only write in German, I can probably use transla-tion web sites to figure out what they're saying.

And what city does your father live in? I think you mentioned that he lives in a city near yours.

I have contacted your 2nd cousins Tommy and Lucy and I'm meeting them this Saturday to tell them about you and your siblings and your father.

And of course Lawrence's little great-granddaughter too! I don't know her last name - I assume she and your sister are not also Graf. That's all for now -

Your Aunt,
Martha

I looked forward to the possibility of communicating directly with my other nephew and my nieces (Samuel's siblings), to learn about their lives as well. My new family was ever expanding.

CHAPTER 11

Telling My Rollins Relatives

I was very curious as to whether some of my father's relatives had known about his relationship with a woman in Germany during his time there, and if they knew of his half-German, half-American child. No relative had ever said anything to me that gave me any indication that they had knowledge of this. My much older cousin Donald Rollins had idolized his Uncle Lawrence. I inherited a photo of my father from one of his early leaves. In it, he is standing in uniform at his parents' home and holding the hand of little Donald, about age four or five, who was wearing a tiny uniform that looked similar to Lawrence's. And little Donald was just beaming! When Donald was old enough to go into the military, he did so, and when he finished his service, he evidently enjoyed talking with his Uncle Lawrence about military commonalities.

I called Donald to pick his brain. Perhaps my father had shared some information with his nephew, while bonding over war stories. He was a bit surprised to hear from me out of the blue. We made small talk for a while and then I asked him if he had known that my father had a girlfriend in Europe when he was in the army, at the end of WWII. Donald kind of hemmed and hawed a bit, but eventually admitted that although his Uncle Lawrence had not given him any specifics, he had picked up on hints that he did have a girlfriend while he was in the service.

I then asked Donald, "Did you know that a child was involved?"

His surprised, immediate response was, "No, I didn't know there was a *child* involved!"

I told Donald the story and he told me that I'd just have to get myself and Eric over to Germany to meet these people pronto.

Donald, son of my Uncle Harold, was the oldest *living* member of the original dozen Rollins grandchildren. Because my parents were married for over twenty years before I was born, most of my first cousins, like Donald, were much older than me. In fact, the eldest of the twelve Rollins grandchildren, Leslie, had *children* about my age. Her son Tommy and I had even gone through thirteen years of school together, starting with nursery school. The night of our high school graduation, there were many Rollins family members present, despite the limited number of tickets allotted to each graduate. My grandmother Edna Rollins (who was Tommy's great-grandmother) and my father had naturally received graduation invitations from me. Tommy's grandmother Lucille (my Aunt Lucille), and his mother Leslie had received graduation invitations from Tommy. Edna was able to see both a grandchild (me) and a great-grandchild (Tommy) graduate that evening. My grandfather Albert Rollins had passed away a few years prior but I'm sure he was there in spirit. It was a wonderful celebration for all of us.

Even though I had not seen them as much as I would have liked while growing up, Lucy and Tommy were the closest thing I had to a sister and brother, so I wanted to share my news about my new family members with them. Donald didn't bat an eye at the fact that my father had been unfaithful to my mother, and I felt that Tommy and Lucy wouldn't be judgmental about my dad's past either. But I was still rather nervous when I called Tommy to ask if I might meet with him and his sister to give them some family news.

After reaching both, we agreed to meet at Tommy's house as it was a convenient place for all of us. I brought a box of tissues with me, as I still couldn't get through telling this story without crying. While I enjoyed relating the story, each time I felt overwhelmed with so many emotions that the tears just flowed. I also brought with me some photos of my dad from his time in the military, as well as photos of my brother, and some of the printed emails from Samuel, to show my cousins.

On the designated Saturday, I arrived at Tommy and his wife's home. Lucy, Tommy, and I went into their living room while Tommy's wife made us lunch in the kitchen. I took a deep breath and said, "I wanted to share this information with you both, because you have been the closest thing I ever had to a sister and a brother…until now."

Before I could get any more words out, Lucy broke in and said, "You have a sister."

I slowly replied, "Noooo, I have a half-brother."

She was quiet then and let me continue. I explained that when my father was overseas during WWII, "he was stationed in Germany when the war was over, to help with the reconstruction of that country. And even though he was married to my mother at the time, he had had a relationship with a German woman, and had fathered a child – a baby boy. But the baby boy wasn't born until November of 1946, and my father had been discharged from the army in May of 1946, so Daddy never got to see his baby son, or hold his baby son, or know his son growing up. But he did know about the boy. And my mother also knew about the boy, and evidently my mother was adamant that I never know this 'horrible scandalous secret.'"

I distributed the photos of my father during his army years and then showed them photos of my brother, and they could see the resemblance unquestionably. Tommy then spoke up and said, "As my sister started to say, our mother told us shortly before she died that you had a sister."

I was shocked. Tommy and Lucy had learned that I had a sibling but had never told me? And their mother Leslie knew something about this, having told them when she was near death from cancer in 1994?

The fact that they had the gender of my sibling wrong had to have come from Leslie's mother Lucille, my dad's older sister. Lucille often got details wrong, and my mother would sometimes sputter about, "Lucille told us the wrong time for the birthday party" or, "Lucille told us the wrong cemetery for the burial," etc. My father was pretty close with his sisters Lucille and Gloria, so it doesn't surprise me that he had shared with at least one (if not both) of them that he had a child with another woman. And so probably his older sister Lucille got the child's gender wrong when sharing this secret with her daughter Leslie. Evidently Leslie wanted her kids to be able to help me in some way, should I ever find out about my sibling, and she passed along to them what information she had been told.

It wasn't Tommy's or Lucy's place to tell me this secret. In fact, since they thought I had a sister, it would have been terrible if they had told me this wrong information, and I had spent time and effort searching for a sister that never existed.

That's the only information that my eldest first cousin Leslie had told her children – that Uncle Lawrence had a child with another woman, and that the child was a female. But there was no information about it happening during his time in the military. Both Lucy and Tommy said that they had scanned the crowd at my dad's funeral back in 1997 to see if they noticed anyone in attendance who appeared to be out of place. They assumed that this unknown-to-me sister would have learned about Lawrence's funeral and that she would be in attendance. They had not forgotten what their dying mother had told them a few years prior to my dad's passing.

Over the next few weeks I reached out to some of my other Rollins cousins, to tell them that they had a newly found cousin. I called my cousin Bobby, who was the son of my Aunt Darlene, and told him that I had recently learned I have a half-brother in Germany. Bobby seemed rather surprised at his Uncle Lawrence being unfaithful to Aunt Rose, but was not at all surprised that my dad had told my mom about the situation. When I told Bobby on the phone that my mother knew about the boy, Bobby's response was "Of course she did – Uncle Lawrence would have told her." My cousins all looked up to my dad and thought very highly of him. Unfortunately, several of these cousins had passed away by this point – from cancer or heart attacks or complications from Alzheimer's. But I reached out to those who were left, to update them on our family tree. Some did not respond back to my efforts to contact them, while others wished me well in getting to know my new family members.

CHAPTER 12

Learning More

It had been less than two months after the initial email arrived from Samuel, and he and I were already sharing information about our lives on a regular basis. Each new message from my nephew would make me smile.

June 2, 2014 –

Hallo Martha,

my job interview went good, anyway i haven't got an answer yet. They told me that they'll make a decision this week. We'll see.

Yesterday i met my dad. Told him about all the things you wrote and showed him the pictures you sent. I think he is glad thta i found you, he told me that he is proud that i ever was so interested in this unknown part of my family. But he is not an such emotional type of human. But he said that he feeld like he has also to write you, so i gave him your email address. Maybe his wife can help him a bit writing in english, otherwise he is gonna write in german. Hope google translater can help :-) but he gave me a picture that he wants me to show you, its him in 2012 with his new wife when he was in New York City. It has been the first time he travelled to the US.

My father lives in Lippstadt, the city i grew up. Both of my parents live there. My brother moved back to Lippstadt with his wife last year after living in Bielefeld for almost 5 years. And my sister moves back to

Lippstadt in July, too. She lived in several cities due to her college and work but comes back now with her husband and daughter. Lawrence's great granddaughters name is Sonja. Her last name is Neumann.

You saw the pictures of my "parents in law" in facebook. But you're right, Marla and i are not married yet. I just used this term because it was easier for me. My webcam arrived, i try to install it today after work.

WIsh you a nice day!

Take care,
yours Samuel

Hi Samuel,

Thank you for the new photograph and the wonderful news that my brother Rolf intends to e-mail me!!

I'm so excited to hear from him!

And thank you for your other information too.

I'm at work right now, so I don't have much time to respond, but I'm really looking forward to Skyping with you and to hearing from Rolf.

Yours -
Martha

A few days later, in early June, Samuel sent me a request through Skype for my contact information, so that we could actually see and hear each other and talk via video chat. We shared contact information and scheduled a time to do this a couple of days later. I was extremely excited to do this long-distance meeting of my father's grandson.

On June 22, 2014, Samuel and I were both signed in to Skype at 2:30 p.m. my time, which was 8:30 p.m. his time. Samuel sent me a message asking if he could video call me in about ten minutes and I responded yes! I went into the bathroom to brush my hair and check how I looked. I was giddy that I was about to meet my nephew and so I wanted to make a good first impression (although his real first impression of me was already obtained from our emails).

I waited with anticipation for him to call, and my heart was pumping fast when I heard the "boop-bee-boop" sound of the video call coming in on my computer. I answered and we excitedly, happily, and a little nervously, greeted each other. He had sent me a photo of himself with his girlfriend, so I knew that he was a nice-looking young man. But when I saw him on the video chat, I was surprised how handsome he really was. But one of the first things he said to me was to apologize for wearing a hat in our initial video meeting; he said that he was having a bad hair day. He used different words to describe it but that was what he meant. I couldn't help but laugh and tell him that I had just brushed my hair before his call.

Later after the video call, I thought back on how my dad had spent many minutes each morning attempting to get his limited amount of hair to look as good as possible. "I'm primping" he'd jokingly say in a silly voice, whenever I'd tease him about how much time he was spending in front of the mirror fixing his hair.

Samuel and I talked about what we had each done that day, and the weather where we each were. He explained how he had searched on the internet for a long time before finding much of anything about the name Lawrence Rollins, and I explained how excited I was to learn of my dad's other child and his grandchildren, and even a little great-granddaughter. I had so many questions for him.

One of the most important facts he reiterated to me was that my brother Rolf didn't speak very much English. I knew if I wanted to visit Germany and meet my brother one day, I would first need to learn enough German to be able to have a conversation with those who didn't speak much English, however brief it might be. Just learning a few words here and there would not cut it. I did not want to stare blankly at my brother upon meeting him, unable to communicate with him. Flying all that way across the Atlantic Ocean only to sit and stare at each other wordlessly was not acceptable to me. And I did not want to impose on others to sit and translate for me the entire time. Plus, my little grandniece would not learn English in school for several more years. And I wanted to be able to connect with her as well.

Our call lasted for nearly forty-five minutes, as we shared information about ourselves and our families – me sharing information about my father, and Samuel sharing information about his father and his siblings. I tried to speak as clearly as I could, and to speak rather slowly, enunciating clearly, as I knew that English was not the language he used the most. But he spoke it very well and I was able to understand him easily, although I could tell it was British English that he had learned. For example, he referred to the place he lived as his "flat" rather than his apartment.

He described how he had only lived with his dad for a few years when he was very young, as his parents had divorced early in his life. He mentioned his mother and told me that her name was, of all the coincidences, Rose. That was my mother's name as well. I was astonished to learn this! Both Lawrence and his son had married women named Rose. And Samuel's older brother's name was Erik, very much like my husband Eric. Another strange coincidence of names – Daddy had both a son-in-law named Eric and a grandson named Erik.

I wondered if my dad realized when Eric and I shared our happy news of being engaged that he would have a son-in-law named Eric, and a grandson in Germany named Erik. After all, that letter from my brother to Daddy had arrived at my parents' home in 1986, about a year before Eric and I met. And in with that letter was a snapshot of my brother, his wife Rose and their eldest two children, Christina and Erik. Even if Daddy didn't make *that* name connection, I'm certain that he must have been floored to learn that his long-lost son had married a woman named Rose. If my mother read that also, she must have felt disgusted.

During our call, I could sense that Samuel was a bit nervous, and he kept reaching for a glass of what appeared to be water, just off camera. It reminded me of how nervous I was in my job interview for my present position, and how I kept asking for another glass of water during the several hours of questioning. I wondered if this parched throat during nervous times, and concern with how our hair looked before meeting someone new, were just normal human reactions for anyone, or genetic traits that were passed down from my father to his offspring. I too was a bit nervous in talking with my nephew, but I think he was more nervous whereas I was more thrilled. After a half-hour or so, our conversation no longer flowed as easily, as we really did not know each other very well. We decided to end our conversation but agreed that we would have another video call soon.

There were no German language courses offered at the nearby university during times that I could attend. I was unable to find any online German language courses from other colleges and universities that seemed affordable. So I purchased a software package to learn German on my own.

Starting that summer, I would get up about half-hour to forty-five minutes early most mornings and spend some time before work learning and practicing the lessons. It seemed to go so slowly. There were times when I got very frustrated with myself trying to learn these new words and phrases. I would see a photo and hear a voice speaking about that photo; first it was just a single word, like *girl* or *apple* or *grass*. Then adjectives and verbs were introduced, so that I could say "The grass is green" and "The girl swims" in German. I was tested in reading, listening, speaking, and writing German, and I was positively the worst at writing. But I could not move on to the next lessons if I did not meet a minimum standard on the previous lesson in all four areas.

There were times that I wanted to cry, or throw the laptop across the room, as I would get so frustrated. No one that I knew (in this country) was able to help me practice speaking and listening to German, so I had to rely strictly on the software. The half-hour live interactive sessions with a native German language speaker were very helpful for me in preparing for our trip.

I was so full of excitement and anticipation at the thought of communicating with my new German family members that I had this burning desire to work on my German language most days for a full eighteen months, from June 2014 until December 2015. I wanted to put forth as much effort as I could, to be able to show my German family members that I wanted very much to communicate with them. Even though most of them would be able to converse with me in English since many had been taught (British) English in school, my brother and my little grandniece would probably not be able to do so. And who knew how often I might need to use German to speak with strangers during our time in Germany.

Samuel and I emailed every few days at first; we had so many questions to ask each other. He mentioned that if he could find an inexpensive flight, he might try to come in August for a quick visit, which made me very excited to think I might meet one of my father's descendants so soon. We scheduled another video chat for mid-summer, and this time we were a bit less nervous.

Despite my father leaving behind his son, that son turned his difficult childhood (growing up in war-ravaged Germany in the late 1940s and the 1950s) into the opportunity as an adult to help young children in need. And he had passed along this calling to both of his sons. I was heartened just imagining the many young German children who had been helped by my dad's son and grandsons.

Some people might say that my father abandoned his son, but he didn't really have much choice. He was in the military and was required to return home to the United States. He couldn't afford to pay for a return visit to Germany, and his whole family (wife, parents, siblings) were all here in the States. From what Samuel had told me about his grandmother, she returned to Berlin to live with her parents before her baby was born. I believe that my dad did not know how to reach Gretchen to offer support, until he came across her letters that my mother had intercepted.

I continued to wonder what my brother's thoughts were about this situation, now that he knew he had a sister, and that sister was raised by "Lawrence Rollins and his wife." I kept telling myself that Daddy was usually a quiet man, and not terribly communicative so perhaps that trait had been passed down to his son, and that Rolf wasn't upset but just wasn't quite sure what to say to me yet. I kept myself busy with my full-time job, my early mornings working on German, exercising at the gym after work a few times each week, and weekend activities with Eric.

CHAPTER 13

My First Message from My Brother

Rolf's first email to me wasn't until July 22, 2014. It seemed like it took forever for him to reach out to me. But I was very excited to read his message when it finally arrived.

July 22, 2014
Subject: sister and brother

Dear Martha,

I am very pleased that my son Samuel has made "my" American family identified. Suddenly I have a sister (and you have a brother) and after about 66 years, a picture of my father. My mother told me very little of my (our) father, to wich I had a letter no information. I have and still always had a positive image of the United States, perhaps a small inheritance. 2012 I was with my wife Seraphina an stepdaugters Annika und Lettie in New York, a great city! How far ist N. Y. away from you? Your probably some rural and quiet lives! What profession practiced than our father out, he was engaged socially and politically? How close is because your family life his aunts and uncles? Just write times on your daily life. I myself am no longer work, but

active in several social organizations an in a political party. Also, I
have a big family!

> *kind regards*
> *Rolf*

My adrenaline went through the roof when I saw that I had an email from my newly found brother. I was thrilled to finally receive a message from him. And although the English was broken, they were kind words – no harsh tones. In my first reading of his email, I was a bit miffed that in his first few lines of communication, it seemed that he was seeking "an inheritance" from our father. But then I thought perhaps I am not interpreting his meaning correctly; after all, there is a language barrier between us, unfortunately. There must be numerous instances in which one German word could have several possible translations in English. Maybe his meaning was more "an inherited trait," rather than a financial inheritance. And I assumed that someone must have helped him write this in English, as Samuel had told me that his father didn't know much English. It is conceivable that the word "inheritance" has a less-financial focus to someone learning British English than it does to those born in the United States. But my initial interpretation of his wording was still at the forefront of my mind as I composed my reply email. Still, I was very happy to write back to my brother right away.

Dear Rolf,

Something deep inside me told me to check my emails this morning before leaving to go to work, and I am SO glad that I did because I saw your message to me!! Thank you for writing and for letting me know that you are interested in connecting with me and for learning more about our father. I am very grateful to Samuel for reaching out to me in April and informing me of you all - eine Familie - (I just learned that German phrase last night). I had no idea of your existence!

I had to laugh out loud when I read of your thoughts regarding a 'small inheritance'. Our father was a wonderful man, very funny and honest, but "Ambitious" is not a description of him. He worked for the State Highway Department for many years after I was born.

When he first got back to the U.S. after the army, I guess he bounced around from job to job a lot. While growing up, I did not realize that we were rather poor - we always had a nice house, plenty to eat, and my mother made my clothes to wear. But there was no money for any sort of vacations, they had no money to send me to college, and after my mother could no longer live at home alone in 2007, I had to sell the house I grew up in to pay for her care.

I'm going to be late for work now, so I must end this message. But thank you again for writing to me. I will definitely write again very soon.

I must warn you that while I am trying to learn German, the writing of it is my worst of all.

Take care -
Your sister – Martha

I was on cloud nine the rest of that day, and for the next several days, knowing that my brother had reached out to me and wanted to know more about me and our father.

A couple of weeks later, I decided to try writing an email to my brother, this time in German (with what I was intending to say also written in English below my German text). I wanted to know more about my brother's family and their birthdays, important dates, and so on. I felt like he would be OK with my emailing him, now that he had initiated an email to me. I hoped that my message to him would be written well enough that he could understand it, but I had included the English version in case someone needed to help him because the German might not be correct.

Guten Tag Rolf,
Wie geht's?
Ich scribe:
Haben sie ein Auto?
Haben sie eine Katze?
Haben sie einen Hund?
Ich haben zwei grau auto - 2009 Pontiac G6 und 2001 Chevrolet Camaro.

Google Translate:

Aber mein Camaro hat viel Rost.

Ich kann nicht fahren es viel länger.

Das macht mich traurig.

Ich liebe mein Camaro.

Ja, wenn unser Vater war lebendig und gut, er war fast 2 seiner Schwestern und seinem Bruder. So sah ich sie ziemlich oft.

Aber jetzt, dass sie tot sind , habe ich nur selten sehen, ihre Kinder, meine Cousins.

Wie oft haben Sie Ihre Kinder sehen? Und Ihre Enkelin?

> *Tschüss,*
> *Martha*

Good Day Rolf,

How are you?

I write:

Do you have a car?

Do you have a cat?

Do you have a dog?

I have 2 grey cars: a 2009 Pontiac G6 and a 2001 Chevrolet Camaro.

From Google Translate -

But my Camaro has much rust.

I won't be able to drive it much longer.

That makes me sad.

I love my Camaro.

Yes, when our father was alive, he was close to 2 of his sisters and his brother. So I saw them quite often.

But now that they are dead, I rarely see their children, my cousins.

How often do you see your children? And your granddaughter?

> *Bye -*
> *Martha*

Later at work, I told my colleague Lilith about my new-found family. Lilith and I had worked together, although in different departments, for many years and I felt that I could trust her with this information. While part of me wanted to shout from the rooftops that "I have a brother!" another part of me felt that this long-held secret should only be shared with people I trusted to not be too judgmental. Physically Lilith had always reminded me of my maternal grandmother – very slender and petite, with wire-rimmed glasses and grayish hair pulled up into a bun. And her voice even reminded me of Gramma's. So when her immediate response to my story was "Oh what a horrible ordeal for your mother!" it struck me that this must have been a similar but much more muted version of my grandmother's reaction to learning what her daughter was experiencing.

Just a few hours later, I checked my home email address and saw that Rolf had responded to my email, and it was all in German. This made me very happy to see, that he seemed to be able to understand what I had written to him, and he felt comfortable enough to respond in his own language. He shared the birthdays of each of his family members and the date he and his current wife married. He also shared that they had no dog or cat and that their car was a VW Golf. That weekend I wrote all the dates of my new relatives in my birthday book and on the calendar, so that I could start preparing to send cards at the appropriate times.

When we discussed going to Germany to meet my new family, Eric said that it would be preferable for at least one of *them* to come *here* to meet on *our* turf, before we traipse halfway across the world to meet people we don't know at all. I agreed. I hoped that at least one of my German family members would come to visit us in the coming months.

Summer progressed, and Samuel's musings about visiting the United States in late summer did not come to pass. But he indicated that he and his girlfriend Marla planned to spend New Year's Eve in New York City and then visit Boston and lastly come up to Maine to meet Eric and me. I was thrilled at this prospect.

Samuel sent me a few more photos of his (and now my) family members, including several of his little niece (my grandniece) Sonja. One of the photos of two-year-old Sonja, taken a few months prior, looked *a lot* like I did at that age. In fact, I rummaged through the old photo album of my childhood and found a Christmas card with my photo on it when I was about a year old, sitting at my mother's piano. I was propped up on pillows on top of the piano bench, with my hands out as if I were getting ready to play a song on the instrument. My face in that photo, when compared with one of the photos of my little grandniece, looked very much alike. I felt a real connection to this little girl who resembled me, knowing that I would never have a daughter of my own. Those photos promptly went up on the hidden side of my file cabinet at work, so that I could see them readily but others entering my office could not.

In late August Samuel and I had another Skype video chat, and he thanked me for the birthday card that we had sent to him. He said that he was so happy to hold something in his hands that I had held in my hands. This made me feel really special and appreciated. He helped with some of my German language questions, and we talked about his and Marla's recent vacation to the northern part of Germany.

On a mid-September Friday afternoon, I had taken a vacation day and I was sitting in front of my laptop. I had Skype open, just in case Samuel wanted to call me... and he did. His girlfriend Marla was with him at his apartment, so I was able to meet her as well. She seemed a bit shy and spoke so softly that I had difficulty hearing her, but I was able to understand her say that it was wonderful I was so accepting of all of them. Samuel wanted to confirm their visit dates with me as they were booking their flights. My hope for meeting them soon was renewed.

CHAPTER 14

Meeting the Family Via Video

As summer slipped into autumn, Samuel and Marla finalized their travel plans, and Samuel emailed me that they had booked their flight to New York City, arriving on December 31st. They would spend New Year's Eve in New York City and would be there several days sightseeing, then head up to Boston to spend several days with Marla's close girlfriend Nora. They would then come and spend a long weekend visiting with us. This would give us an initial meeting— on our home turf, as Eric had suggested— and give my husband and me the chance of getting to know some of this newfound family. Then we could decide about making the commitment to travel to Germany.

In November, I decided that I would email to Rolf and Samuel a couple of old photos of Daddy while he was in Germany after the war. This would be the best I could do for a birthday present for my newly found brother. I had no idea of his likes and dislikes, so I hoped that some photos of where our dad had spent time while in my brother's home country might be interesting for him. I felt certain it would be appealing to Samuel, and perhaps if Rolf had questions, he could go through Samuel to ask me them.

In one of the photos, Daddy was standing shoulder to shoulder with two other guys in U.S. army uniforms, a fellow Private on one side and a Captain on the other. The photo was close enough and clear enough that a lighter line could be seen on Daddy's left hand ring finger. To me, it was obvious that Daddy had worn his wedding ring when he went overseas and was wearing it in that photo. I felt certain that my dad had not kept secret his marital status from anyone in Germany – including Gretchen. I did not mention this in my email to Rolf and Samuel. Instead, I relayed where the bridge he was working on in two different photos was located, according to his army yearbook. The next morning when I got up and turned on my computer to check my emails, I had emails from both Samuel and Rolf. Each had thanked me for the photos that I had sent. I was just thrilled that both seemed very happy to receive them.

As the fall crept on, I started to think about what gifts I could send to my new German family members for Christmas. I wanted them to know about Daddy, and when I saw maple-glazed pecans being sold at our local farmer's market, I decided that would make a great present for each of them. Since Daddy loved maple syrup and had some nearly every day during my childhood and adolescence, and his favorite flavor of ice cream was maple walnut, this would give his German descendants a taste of what he liked to eat. And they wouldn't be terribly expensive to mail overseas.

I also wanted to be able to have my brother see and hear our father, and the only way to do that now that my dad was deceased was to make a copy of Eric's and my wedding video and send that to Rolf and his family. There were several spots in the video of our wedding reception where Daddy spoke, and naturally we also had our father/daughter dance. I just really wanted to share as much information about Daddy with his son and grandson as possible.

And because Christmas is much more special for children than for most adults, I wanted to send a toy to my little grandniece, who would turn three years old just a few days after Christmas. But I did not want to assume sending a gift to the child would be OK, so first I wanted to get permission from my niece Christina, Sonja's mother. Eric regularly told me during this time "Don't force yourself on these people." Since I was so exuberant about these new family members, I did tend to charge forward with efforts to learn about them. But I also realized that I needed to be a bit restrained.

I emailed Christina to ask permission to send a little something to Sonja for Christmas, after obtaining her email from Samuel. And I got her OK as long as it wasn't "too much." At this same time, I also learned that some Germans, like her, check their emails only about once per week, which is very different than most people in the United States.

I went to my maternal cousin Rhonda's crafts fair that she held every year and found a cute rag doll that I thought would be perfect for my grandniece for a Christmas present. I also went to a local photography shop and had our VHS wedding video transferred to a DVD for Eric and me, and also transferred to two DVDs that were supposed to be compatible with many European DVD players. These would be for Rolf and Samuel for Christmas, so that they could not only see our wedding, but also see Daddy moving and speaking at our wedding reception. I wrapped each of these items and found a box to pack everything into, and then prepared the box for shipping to my brother's home.

I was a bit taken aback at the expense of shipping these few, lightweight items, but made the mental note to take this expense into consideration moving forward. I wanted to be sure that these items would arrive in time for my brother and his family's gathering to celebrate Christmas together, which was scheduled to be the Saturday before Christmas. Samuel assured me he would bring his new iPad to the gathering so that he could Skype with me from their event, and so that I could see my brother for the first time. I was thrilled at this idea!

Over and over in my mind, I would play out the scenario as to how this would happen. I imagined my nephew and each of his family members, starting with his father, sitting side by side in front of the iPad so that I could see them readily and ask each of them questions, individually. And each new-to-me family member would answer me, getting assistance from Samuel if needed (because of the language difference). I couldn't wait to have a conversation with my brother.

For weeks this situation consumed my thoughts, and I must have talked about it a great deal at home. Eric had a hard time understanding why I was so excited. His attitude was "Why do you care so much about what these people think? You've lived this long without them."

But I couldn't understand why my husband was so cavalier about the situation. I asked him if he were in a similar situation, wouldn't he want to now know a much older sibling? I reminded him that his mother's first husband had been killed while fighting in WWII, shortly after they got married. What if she had found out she was pregnant after her husband entered the military, learned of his death a few months later, and then had to give up their baby because she couldn't afford to care for it? Wouldn't he want to know that person now if given the opportunity?

He said he didn't think so, which absolutely floored me. I did not understand this view at all. I couldn't *wait* to learn about my new family members. But thankfully, Eric was OK with my desire for him to accompany me to Germany to meet my new family members, especially my brother, before too long. And we had discussed possible times to go, including maybe Christmas time next year *if* the Skype call and upcoming visit from Samuel went well.

As the date of our Skype chat drew nearer, seeing these new family members filled me with anticipation. I hoped that they would like the little gifts I had sent. Samuel had messaged me in early December when the box arrived at his father's home. According to Samuel, my brother Rolf had looked at the delivered package and questioned his wife "now what have you bought?" teasing her about spending too much money, when in fact he had readily seen that it had been shipped from the United States. It sounded like my brother's sense of humor was similar to that of our father. A letter arrived from my eldest nephew Erik, with a photo of him and his bride at their wedding a couple of years earlier. His letter told us a bit about them: She was a pre-school teacher and he was in charge of a daycare center for underprivileged children; he enjoyed sports, and he was pleased to learn about me. Christmas cards arrived in our mail, first from Samuel and then from Rolf and his wife Seraphina.

On the day of our Skype chat, I put on my Christmas sweater and made sure my hair looked OK, as I wanted to do what I could to make a good first impression. The family— my brother and his wife, his four children and their spouses/significant others, and his nearly-three-year-old granddaughter— would all be in attendance. They planned to have their dinner first, and then video call us. I waited on pins and needles for the computer to make the "boop bee, boop bee boop" tone notifying me of an incoming call.

But the agreed-upon time approached, and the call didn't come and didn't come. Finally, after what seemed like ages, but was actually only about twenty minutes, Samuel messaged me via Skype to say that they would make the call in just a couple of minutes.

Then the tone sounded, and I breathlessly accepted the call. When the video started, I could readily see on the screen my nephew Samuel, with little Sonja sitting in his lap. I could clearly see both of them, and Sonja looked a bit puzzled as to how these two people on the screen could interact with her and her uncle. She obviously was not accustomed to video chats with other people, and she knew that people on TV could not see her, like my husband Eric and I were now able to do on *this* screen right now. She didn't say anything, even when prompted by her Uncle Samuel and her mother Christina.

Eric joined me and we sat in chairs close together, so that everyone would be able to see the both of us. Samuel then apologized for the delay in calling, saying it had taken them a bit longer to finish their dinner than he had originally anticipated. "But we are *all* here!" Samuel said, as he slowly panned the iPad around so that we could try to see all ten of the adults sitting at the table. Then he set up the iPad at the end of the long dining table, and I quickly realized that we would be "sitting" at one end of the long table, while everyone else was seated around it.

Unfortunately, this meant that there was quite a distance between the iPad and my brother and his wife, who were sitting at the other end of the table. They were quite fuzzy on my computer screen, and my brother was rather quiet. Evidently the Wi-Fi connection at my brother's house was rather weak in that room, or some other technical issue, because we were not able to see the people sitting around the long table nearly as clearly as we were able to see Samuel and little Sonja when the iPad was set up right in front of the two of them. While I was still very pleased to be able to meet everyone, this was not the set-up I had envisioned over and over in my head.

I did get a brief introduction to each of them, and I was able to ask what they did for work. Sometimes Samuel had to repeat what they had said, either because they spoke too softly for us to hear them, or because their accents made it difficult for Eric and me to understand what they were saying. After receiving an initial bit of information about each one, I was able to ask in German what they liked to do, to which most of the young people in the room answered "sports," and my brother answered comically "essen und trinken" which is German for "to eat and drink." There was the Rollins' sense of humor coming through already. My nephew Erik said that they like to play as well as watch sports, and as everyone in the room was quite slender, I could tell that there were no couch potatoes in this family. I inquired of Rolf about his consulting work and what it entailed, with Samuel translating my question and then Rolf's answer. Then I asked my brother if his mother had spoken English and he responded no, in a way that made me feel I should not ask more questions about his mother during this first interaction.

I asked Rolf's youngest daughter, Lorraine, what she liked and she said horses. Samuel had told me the least amount of information about her, and so I had more questions for her. Lorraine's mother was a different person than Rolf's first wife, the mother of his three older children. I asked Rolf's wife Seraphina if she worked outside of the home, and she said yes, in administration for the government. Next I asked her how she met Rolf, and her response included what sounded like the word "chef," so I repeated back my question "He was your chef?" This seemed incredible to me, as Daddy rarely cooked anything, with the exception of grilling meat on the barbeque. But Seraphina then clarified that no, he was her boss (which in German is *chef* and pronounced the same). Everyone chuckled at this language confusion.

Rolf's eldest daughter Christina then spoke up and asked us the dates of our birthdays, and I told her. Then they asked Eric and me what we knew about Germany. I answered that I knew that Germany had the best economy in Europe, which met with silence. Eric, an avid auto racing fan, then spoke up and said, "All I know about Germany is the Nürburgring," to which they responded "Ah, the Nürburgring! That's not far from here!" And since the Skype call seemed to be going well, I tentatively mentioned that perhaps we could go see it someday. They asked if we had ever been to Europe and we said no, we had only been to Canada for our honeymoon but never to any overseas country.

Then I hesitatingly said, "But... we were thinking about... maybe... visiting Germany next Christmas" and they all (except Rolf who had not understood me) started to clap. They were obviously pleased with this news and seemed very open to the idea, which thrilled me. Immediately after telling my brother what I had said, my sister-in-law replied that they had plenty of room and we could stay with them. But I quickly responded with thanks very much and we greatly appreciate the offer, but we would plan to stay at a hotel, and didn't want to impose on them. They told us that there were very few options for hotels in their small city, but that Cologne was not far and there were many hotels there to choose from as well. I said that we definitely wanted to spend some time getting to know each and every one of them during our visit. I didn't want to insult my brother and his wife by insisting on staying in a hotel rather than with them. But Eric and I preferred to have some breathing room with these people, who were, after all, still strangers to us.

After a good half-hour of Skype conversation, little Sonja was running around the room, asking (in German, naturally) about opening presents. Samuel told us that they had tickets to all go to a concert in which a friend of Rolf's was performing, so they didn't have a lot of time left before they would have to leave. Thus it was the perfect time to accommodate Sonja's wish to open presents and have them open the package I had sent. Samuel maneuvered his iPad so that I could observe Sonja (with her mother's help) open her doll, to which her mother Christina said to Sonja, while holding the dolly up in front of her, "Hello! I am your American friend." And then to me, Christina said "This is very appropriate for her age, thank you." Sonja wasn't quite sure what to make of the doll at first, and the clarity of the video was not terribly good. But we could make out that the first thing she did was poke the doll's belly, which made me laugh out loud. She seemed a bit hesitant at first, but after a few minutes, Samuel showed me via his iPad that Sonja was hugging her new dolly, which made me very pleased.

Then each of the five couples opened their bag of maple glazed pecans, and Lorraine read aloud my note explaining why I had chosen this as a gift (since New England is noted for maple syrup, and Daddy loved maple). I asked if they had maple syrup there in Germany and Erik responded "No, not really." Then Samuel and Rolf each opened their copy of our wedding DVD, to which I had attached our wedding invitation which we had left over from twenty-five-plus years ago. I told them that these DVDs were supposed to work in many European DVD players.

As their time to leave was drawing near, they all gathered together and faced the iPad propped up on the table and sang the German Christmas song "Au Tannenbaum" for Eric and me. I had learned to play this song on the piano as a little girl many years ago, and so I was very familiar with the tune, but not the German lyrics. My eyes welled up with tears as this group sang to us. It was such a lovely moment for me, to be welcomed by this big new family.

CHAPTER 15

Samuel and Marla's Visit

I was so excited to have had a chance to see and speak to each of my German family members, even if the clarity of the video had not been stellar. That video visit with my whole German family was the start of the holiday celebration for Eric and me.

On New Year's Eve day Samuel emailed me when they were safely in New York City, and the next day he messaged me that they had not expected it to be so cold. They had anticipated seeing fireworks at midnight like what is done in the larger cities in Germany on New Year's Eve. I told them that often it is too cold and windy for such things in the Northeastern part of the United States at New Year's.

As the next days passed, they let us know that their friend had rented a car and would drive them from Boston up to the city closest to us, and we could meet at a well-known diner just off the highway in the afternoon of Friday the 9th. I took that Friday and Monday off from work, to prepare for their arrival, and to spend as much time with them as possible. Since Samuel and his girlfriend are vegetarians, I found a vegetarian recipe to cook in the crockpot. I spent time cleaning up the house to make it presentable. Samuel emailed that he would text me as they narrowed in on a time for us to meet at the diner. The afternoon dragged for me, as I anxiously awaited Samuel's text. I had hoped to spend about half the day on Friday with them, but the afternoon was slipping away.

Finally, around 3:00, Samuel texted me that they would be ready to meet in an hour. (Little did I realize that at this moment Samuel was working up his courage to go through with our meeting, he was so nervous about it.) Eric and I headed to the diner, and I was filled with excited anticipation. Would they like us? Would we get along with them? Would we inadvertently do anything to offend them? As I drove us there, these thoughts ran through my mind, and Eric agreed that he would drive us back home, so that I could totally focus on talking with our guests.

When we arrived, my heart was beating rapidly, and I was filled with nervous anticipation. I texted him to let them know where we were parked. Soon they pulled in and all piled out of the rental car. Samuel had a big smile on his face as he approached me to give me a big hug. He was very tall, much taller than I had expected, slender, with long legs, twinkling dark eyes, and a winning smile. His girlfriend was very pretty, very slender, and while shorter than Samuel, she too was taller than both Eric and me. She also gave us each a hug and introduced us to her girlfriend Nora, who I thanked for bringing them to us. We all went inside the diner for a beverage and to warm up a bit.

The conversation was a little bit tentative. Samuel and his girlfriend said that his older sister Christina was correct – that there was a resemblance between her and me. Evidently after our Skype video call with the whole family a few weeks ago, Christina had mentioned to her family after the call that she thought I looked a bit like her. No one else there in Rolf's home saw the resemblance at that time. But now that Samuel and Marla were sitting at a table with me, they said they could see that resemblance.

Marla asked what we thought when Samuel first emailed that he was the grandson of Lawrence Rollins. I replied that I got very angry with Samuel because I felt certain that he was a scam artist. Neither Marla nor Samuel were familiar with this expression, and they looked to Nora to translate that. Both knew the word *artist* but that word did not make any sense in this context. Nora had picked up on various expressions and slang such as this during her months working in Massachusetts as an au pair. Once they understood what I meant, I told them that it took seeing the handwriting and signature on the letter, and then seeing photos of Rolf, for me to believe that Samuel was providing me with truthful information.

We chatted with the three young people for about forty-five minutes and then I mentioned that the supper I had in the crockpot was ready for us at home, and we should get going. Marla's girlfriend was visibly sorry to hear this, as she was sad at the thought of saying good-bye again to her friend. She knew it would be months before they could hang out together again. But the girls said their tearful good-byes, while Eric and Samuel worked to load the suitcases into our car.

The bags were so large that only one fit into the trunk, and the other had to stand upright between the two young people in the back seat. Between helping with their luggage and driving us back, I was very glad that Eric had decided to come along. We went to the hotel to get them checked in and drop off their luggage in their room, which turned out to be a suite. I had done some business with that hotel previously, and so they automatically upgraded my room reservation to the available suite. Samuel and Marla were very surprised to have so much space. It was evidently much more than they were accustomed to when staying away from home.

Immediately Samuel opened his large suitcase and rummaged through it to find the small Christmas gifts that were for us from Samuel and Marla, and from Rolf and Seraphina. Then we brought both them and the gifts to our home. We told them to make themselves comfortable, and Eric gave them a tour of our house while I served up the stew I had made along with some bread. Eric made himself a peanut butter sandwich after tasting the vegetarian concoction. They didn't complain at all (even though it was admittedly a bit bland) and ate it up, as they were hungry.

For dessert I had made my special pumpkin turtle pie, which I had served at the holidays for the last few years and everyone had raved about. So I decided to make it again for this special company. Samuel said that it reminded him a lot of a dessert that his mother Rose had made for him and his older siblings when they were children. I was very happy that I had made a dessert that pleased him.

We all went into the living room to visit in more comfortable seats. Eric and I opened our gifts from Germany, which included cookies in a tin that were all shaped like the Cologne Cathedral, some candies, and some No.4711 brand cologne and shower gel. Samuel asked to see our wedding video, which I had put onto DVDs and sent to him and his dad for Christmas, but unfortunately the DVDs would not play for either Samuel or Rolf in their DVD players. Samuel was quite eager to see a video that included his grandfather walking and talking.

We all watched our wedding video and I identified which relatives were on my Dad's side and which ones were on my Mom's side. And I identified Daddy's younger sister Gloria as my favorite aunt.

By that point, the young couple were getting quite tired, so we decided to wait on looking through the old family photo albums I had dragged out. We brought them back to their hotel room to retire early. But before we did, I showed them a couple of photos of the railroad station where my dad had been born and grown up, as in the morning we'd be heading to Carterville to see that area and other places of significance regarding my dad.

Thankfully the next day was a gorgeous sunny January day. Although cold, there wasn't a cloud in the sky, and almost no wind. We could not have asked for better weather for driving around. We picked the couple up at the hotel around 9:30 the next morning for what I called "Lawrence Rollins Day." For most of the day we would show them places of note and tell them stories about my dad's life. They had eaten some breakfast at the hotel before we got there, and Samuel was quite impressed with their "pancake machine." I had a bunch of specific places in mind to go before it started to get dark, and we headed off toward Carterville.

My father and his siblings had been born and raised in a tiny railroad depot on a dirt road in a small rural town. More freight was delivered there than passengers, and so the storage barn a few steps away from the main building was larger than the depot itself. The first floor held the waiting room and the office where the telegraph machine was located. My grandmother operated the telegraph and sold tickets to the few passengers who boarded there. Upstairs were the living quarters which included three tiny bedrooms, one for my grandparents, one for the boys and one for the girls. Indoor plumbing was not available at this time, and so the outhouse was out back, away from the railroad tracks. Unfortunately, I could not take Samuel and Marla to a similar railroad station, so I decided to take them to the next best thing.

Our first stop was at a little diner in the state capital that was originally an old trolley station, and has a decor similar to an old railroad depot. This was as close as I could come to showing them what my dad's childhood home was probably like. We sipped beverages and chatted more about my dad's childhood.

Then we drove the short distance to one of my employer's campus locations. I think Samuel and Marla were impressed with the fact that I could punch in a code into the keypad and gain access to this nice building on a Saturday when the facility was closed. We didn't stay long, but they had time to admire the high ceilings, skylight, and significant glass in the foyer.

Next, we drove up to the Capital Plaza and stopped in front of the State House. Because it was a weekend, we could not go in, but I explained that my dad had been elected to the State's House of Representatives for two two-year terms. So that was where he had served while in the state legislature. They took photos of each of the buildings that I showed them.

We then drove a couple of blocks to a parking garage and walked to the nearby candy store. I explained that Daddy loved chocolates from there, especially peanut clusters. So whenever it was his birthday or Christmas and I wasn't sure what to get him for a gift, I often got him some candy from there. I bought some of those peanut clusters, and Samuel bought a small container of maple syrup. Samuel had been very interested in the maple glazed pecans that I had sent for Christmas, since they were a favorite of my dad's, although I don't think the others really were all that interested.

We drove up toward Carterville by taking back roads. On the way, I drove in the entrance to a cemetery to try to show the young couple where Lawrence's grandfather Rollins was buried (he died the same year as Lawrence was born – 1917). The roads of the cemetery were not plowed, and I was afraid we might get stuck if I were to stop the car. So we just drove really slowly through the cemetery, but unfortunately I could not locate the exact stone where my great-grandfather and great-grandmother Rollins were buried. But at least Samuel got the feel for that cemetery as we were driving through it.

Afterward we continued to Carterville so that we could see where the depot had been. Tragically it was totally destroyed by a fire in December 1940, and there were very few photos of the depot and barn still in existence. I did have one of those old photos and I brought a copy with us so that I could show the couple how the spot had looked many years ago, to compare it to how it looked today. They were very interested, and then I shared with them the following details.

By the late 1930s, the B&M Railroad no longer needed these two buildings, and my grandfather was able to purchase them. He had the barn moved a few thousand feet away, back farther from the railroad tracks, and he used his woodworking and other skills to convert it into a house for him and my grandmother. By this time, my uncle Harold was grown and married, and so Grandpa was able to sell the smaller depot building to Harold and his wife Iris. By late 1940, Harold and Iris and their baby son Donald were living in the depot when it caught fire and burned to the ground one winter night. While very few of their possessions were salvageable, at least the three occupants of the building were able to escape unharmed. There was even an article in the local newspaper about how Harold had lowered Iris by her arms down from the second story window and then when she was safely on the ground, Harold dropped baby Donald into her waiting arms. Harold was then able to scramble out the window and jump down to the ground to safety.

Grandpa and Grammy Rollins lived comfortably in the barn-turned-house for many years. But by the late 1950s, the interstate highway was being expanded, and the government was able to use eminent domain rules to take the land where Grandpa and Grammy's house now set, paying them for the property. But the government had no use for the house which Grandpa had worked so hard to create into a decent home from just a barn. Grandpa decided to sell the building at auction, to get enough money to purchase a new home, when added to the amount received from the state for the land.

At this time, Lawrence and Rose were living in a small old cape house just a couple of miles away from Grandpa and Grammy's house. In addition to the cape, they also owned the sizable field with a small barn on it across the road. They decided that they would try to purchase Grandpa and Grammy's house at the auction, and have it moved up the road to their field, and then live in this larger house and rent out their small cape. The plan worked. They successfully bought the building at the auction, much to the relief of everyone in the family, knowing that Grandpa's hard work wasn't about to be demolished. My dad hired specialists to move the building, now going through its second relocation, to his property. This former barn was then where my parents lived and was also the house I lived in from the time I was born until I was four years old.

Samuel and Marla listened intently to my story. I then told them that I had a surprise for them. The present owners of this barn-turned-house were the granddaughter of the couple who purchased the house from my parents in the mid-1960's, along with her husband and kids. When I knew which weekend these young Germans would come to visit us, I had gotten word to the present owners that a distant relative of my father's was visiting and would love to see the inside of that house. She and her husband graciously agreed to allow us to come into their home and take a brief tour of the main floor.

I was so happy to be able to show my nephew and his girlfriend inside this house. I texted the woman that we were on our way and when we arrived a few minutes later, Marla took a photo of the house and yard area. The owners welcomed us in, and I immediately recognized the kitchen cabinets and built-in drawers as my grandfather's handiwork. The house hadn't really been changed all that much since Grandpa first created it from the old barn roughly seventy-five years ago. I just loved seeing it.

Eric and Samuel and Marla seemed curious to look around this place, but I was the one who was relishing being able to see the old kitchen cupboards and put my hand on the outside of the built-in drawers my grandfather had built so many years ago. Although I had only a couple of very vague memories from living here, I was very happy to be able to spend a few minutes in this house again, and we all thanked the occupants for their kindness.

Our next stop was the house where I had grown up. On our way we drove past the location of the one-room schoolhouse that my dad and his siblings had all attended, and also the farm he worked on when he first left school to help support the family. Samuel was very interested in all of these places. Thankfully the woman I had sold my childhood home to in 2007, Ginger, also graciously agreed to allow us to tour it as well. I had emailed her a couple of weeks before our visitors arrived, to ask if it might be possible to see the place again and she kindly agreed. I honestly wasn't sure how emotional I'd get when entering that house again, as I had not seen it since I had sold it.

When we drove in, Ginger was bringing some firewood in for the wood stove. She greeted us all and brought us into the garage. She told me that when she moved in and was storing some items way up high in the garage she came across an old sign that said "Rollins," which my father had purchased many years ago. I remembered that he had hung it over our mailbox at the end of the driveway for several years, but at one point he had taken it down, and evidently stored it overhead in the garage. Eric and I had not found it when we cleaned out the house for selling. But Ginger, who was a few years ahead of me in school and remembered me, decided to hang it up inside the garage when she came across it.

Samuel requested to have his picture taken next to the sign. Obviously this meant a great deal to him, to be photographed in what had been his grandfather's garage, standing beside a sign with his last name. He seemed so happy to be in his American grandfather's former home. I felt the need to tell Ginger about who this young man was and give her an abbreviated version of our story. She seemed happy to be able to contribute to our adventure on this day. Maybe because of this "transition time" of chatting out in the garage, and seeing how happy Samuel was to be here, I did not get as emotional as I feared I might upon entering my childhood home, which was no longer mine.

We went inside and looked around the kitchen and dining area, and then the living room, stopping at the fireplace. I described how my parents would pop popcorn over fires in it during winters when I was a child. Then we walked down the hallway and peeked in both small bedrooms. I mentioned that Ginger had taken down the blue flowered wallpaper in the corner bedroom, which had been my room. She mentioned how that wallpaper had been particularly challenging for her to remove.

When we went into the master bedroom, I commented on how the wallpaper was still the same as when I had sold the house. Samuel happily asked, "So this was my grandfather's bedroom, with the wallpaper he had?!" I told him yes, although it was not the original wallpaper from that room – my parents had changed it when I was a teenager. But yes, that wallpaper was put up by my parents when they were living here. "Wow!" Samuel softly exclaimed.

As we left, I asked Ginger not to mention this new family situation to anyone else in Carterville and she agreed to keep it our secret. But we all thanked her again for allowing us to tour her home. We could all tell how much Samuel appreciated this opportunity to view his grandfather's former residence.

Next we went to the Carterville center, the closest thing to a "downtown" that existed. The town hall, the church and its parish house, the country store, the library, and the historical society were all located in this town center, along with a cemetery. I had been in the store hundreds of times during my years growing up in this town, and not a lot had changed inside. We all went in so that I could show Samuel and Marla this establishment where my dad had shopped many times.

The post office for the town was also located inside the store. While I don't think the post office was located here when my father used a post office box for a return address to write to Gretchen back in 1951, the boxes appeared to be old enough to still be the same ones from back then. Samuel wanted to take a photo of them. Then we walked to the front of the parish house building, and I described how the upstairs hall had been used for my bridal shower in the late 1980's, and for my parents' fiftieth wedding anniversary party in 1990. And it had also been the hall used for their twenty-fifth wedding anniversary party, when I was four years old. Not only that, it had also been the location for my Grandpa and Grammy Rollins' fiftieth wedding anniversary party when I was just a little tot. So many of our family's big events were held in that building.

Also located in the town center was a tall granite marker dedicated to the town's veterans of all wars. My dad had been instrumental in getting this stone created and placed, and Samuel wanted photos taken of him and me, and then him and Marla, standing next to it. In years gone by, there were many winter days with so much snow on the ground that the bottom third of the marker had been covered in the white stuff. Thankfully there was not a lot of snow on the ground this year, and Samuel's photos showed most of the stone.

Next we headed toward the cemetery where my parents are buried, driving by the elementary school I attended for six years. I described how my father occasionally had difficulty driving me up the steep hill in his pick-up truck to the school building when there were icy roads in the winter.

A few minutes later we arrived at the entrance to the cemetery, but the road had not been plowed and the hill was covered in a crusty snow. I was concerned about trying to drive our car up the unplowed road into the cemetery, so I pulled over to the side of the main road and said to the young couple that the hill was a bit treacherous. I told them if they didn't want to walk up the hill that was OK.

Marla looked at me and said, "We've traveled thousands of kilometers for this; we're not going to let a little hill stop us." So we walked up, digging our heels in to the crust as we walked. We got to the section where my parents, my grandparents, and my Aunt Darlene were buried, and I walked over to my parents' graves. I started brushing the snow off their headstone so that their names were visible, while Samuel and Marla started making their way toward me.

When I had finished cleaning the snow, Samuel stood a bit back from the gravestone and stared at it for a long time. Marla walked over and stood next to him, putting her arm around him and saying something to him softly. I took a photo of them, with the gravestone in front of them and the small American flag sticking out of the snow at the back edge of the plot. At first Samuel's face had a slight smile, as his long quest to learn about his American grandfather was finally over, and he was actually now standing there at his grandfather's grave.

As he looked at the gravestone I heard him say, "You can be at peace now— we are together." Then his expression slowly changed to sorrow. I could tell that Samuel was starting to cry, and it surprised me that this stranger was getting so emotional over my dad's grave site. But obviously he had spent quite a bit of time over his life thinking about and wondering about his American grandfather. It meant a great deal to him that I had brought him to this place.

Samuel asked Marla to take a couple of photos of him standing near the grave, pointing to the name on the grave, and brushing snow off the military plaque next to the little American flag. He absolutely wanted keepsake photos from this location.

Soon the sun was starting to sink down below the trees, and it was getting colder, so it was time for us to carefully make our way back down the slippery hill. Marla walked behind Samuel and me and got a really nice photo of us descending the snow-covered hill while the setting sun shone down on us. We got back to the car and I passed around a box of tissues, as there were still a few tears amongst us.

Eric drove us towards a restaurant near our home, while I asked the young people questions about themselves and the whole family. Samuel said that his grandmother Gretchen had moved to Berlin shortly before Rolf was born and lived with her father and two sisters. At one point there was evidently a very full apartment with Gretchen and little Rolf, her two sisters, the daughter of one of those sisters, and Gretchen's father all living there. Rolf's grandfather had been his male role model while growing up. So even though Gretchen never married, there was a fatherly figure in his life. Rolf had entered the German army right after completing school, and it was while he was serving that his mother Gretchen was diagnosed with cancer, and unfortunately passed away at a young age.

Rolf and Rose divorced when Samuel was quite young, so Samuel has no memories of living with both of his parents. His older siblings Christina and Erik do, Samuel said, but he was too young to remember. At one point I asked Samuel what his favorite memory of his father was, and that caused him to ponder for a while. Finally, he said that the vacation trips that he and his dad had taken when he was a boy were his favorite memories of time they had spent together.

Soon we arrived at the restaurant. After we gave the waiter our orders, I pulled out a small notebook from my purse and began writing down what I would be eating for supper. As Samuel and Marla observed me writing down what I would be eating, they stared at me and then looked at each other, and then back at me. Samuel asked me "Your write down what you eat?" and I explained that yes, I track what I eat, as a long-time Weight Watchers member, to help me be accountable of my food intake.

Samuel then replied, "My dad writes down what he eats also!" I asked Samuel if his father had ever had a problem with his weight, and he responded that no, Rolf had never been heavy. Obviously, this food tracking habit was a rather unusual one for most people in both German and American cultures, and the fact that my brother and I had this in common, despite never knowing each other, seemed rather unusual to all four of us at the table.

After our meal we all went back to our house so that we could enjoy another piece of my homemade pie and look at the old photo albums of pictures of my parents and their families. There was one photo of Lawrence taken in 1951, according to my mother's handwritten date on the margin. He was smiling and sitting in a lawn chair next to his newly built barbeque pit and patting their dog, a collie. Because it was a good photo of him, and it was taken the same year that he had written to Samuel's grandmother, Samuel asked if I'd mind if he took a picture of that photograph with his phone. I told him I didn't mind at all. By the time we got through a couple of photo albums, we were all getting a bit tired since we had gotten an early start that morning. We drove the young couple back to the hotel and planned to take them out to brunch the next morning.

In the morning we all slept in a bit later than we had on Saturday, and Samuel called me to let us know that they were up and nearly ready to go to brunch. We headed over to pick them up and took them to a nearby golf course that served a delicious brunch each Sunday morning. We had a table next to a window with a lovely view of the snow-covered greens below. Our waitress was kind enough to take a photograph of the four of us at the table. It was a lovely time.

Back at home, Eric worked with Samuel to copy our wedding DVD onto a thumb drive. This gave me a chance to talk with Marla upstairs uninterrupted. I told her that I would like her to give a message to my two nieces Christina and Lorraine, since they were descendants of the Rollins family. I told Marla how a few years earlier I had had a close call with cancer. During a necessary surgery, an ovarian tumor was discovered that my doctor said would have most likely turned cancerous had it not been removed promptly. I wanted Marla to tell my two nieces how important it is for them to go see a doctor right away should they have any unusual female symptoms, especially since both their dad's mother and father had died from cancer. Marla assured me that she would tell them. I said I was glad that I could share this with her, to get that information to them, because I wasn't comfortable sharing this with Samuel as he was a guy. She said she understood perfectly, and that she was sure my nieces would appreciate getting this information.

Just then the men came back up to join us, and we looked through more old photographs, including Eric's and my wedding album. We chatted some more and by early afternoon, as the conversation lulled, Eric suggested that we take a drive to the beach. Marla had studied marine biology and was expecting to begin her master's degree in that subject soon, so this was right up her alley. And the Atlantic Ocean was only about an hour's drive away.

Eric drove so that I could focus more on having a conversation with the young people. The morning's sunshine had faded behind thickening clouds, but thankfully it was good driving weather. A cloudy cold day in January meant that we had the beach all to ourselves, which was nice. Marla said that this was the first time she had ever seen snow on the beach. While Germany gets some snow in the winter, New England gets much colder and usually has much more snow and ice than their country ever sees. We walked to keep warm and took pictures of the scenery and each other. Marla seemed to appreciate this opportunity to see the beach in a new way, with snow clinging to some of the rocks. Before too long, we were getting cold and hopped back into the car to head for home, this time taking a less direct route which took us by some gorgeous homes, what some might call mansions.

There was still another hour or so to go before dinner would be ready, so once we got back, I brought out some cheese and crackers for us to munch on while we waited for the meal to finish cooking. This was a very familiar situation for our German visitors – having something to nibble on before the main meal was served. We chatted around the kitchen table, and this felt like the most comfortable we had ever been with each other.

After supper and finishing off the last of the pumpkin turtle pie, we went into the living room again. I popped in the VHS tape of very old black and white reel-to-reel video that my mother's brother Willie had created for Christmas gifts for us several decades before. There was no sound from the video, just music that had been dubbed onto the tape. There were scenes of a Thanksgiving gathering when I was just a little tot, sitting in a highchair at my grandparents' home, along with Willie and his wife and their three kids gathered around the table.

One scene showed Lawrence making sure I was secure in the highchair, and then patting me on the head. There were also scenes from a couple of Christmas gatherings with the same group of relatives. At one point I wanted to play with my brand-new toy xylophone, and the adults were trying to distract me away from that with other quieter toys. Finally, my dad swooped me up and gently set me on the seat of the chalkboard desk/chair and handed me some chalk so that I could draw. The transitions between videos were choppy at times, and there were more scenes of cows than I thought were necessary. But it was certainly a nice keepsake, and Samuel and Marla seemed to appreciate my showing it to them.

When the video had ended, Samuel asked wistfully, "Why couldn't Lawrence have reached out to my father?" I responded, "I wish he *had* connected with Rolf," and I started to cry. Eric started to explain to the young couple that in the 1940s, 1950s, 1960s, and even 1970s, having a baby with someone you were not married to was considered to be a shocking, terrible thing.

Eric told them how *his* father had been warned as a child "Don't play anywhere near that house! The people who live there aren't married!" With each passing decade, society gradually became more accepting of family situations that did not adhere to the traditional married father and mother and their children, and no one else. We both apologized to Samuel for upsetting him by showing that video to them, and Marla quickly apologized to me if anything either of them had said had upset me. I told them that this whole situation has been very emotional for me, so they shouldn't feel bad for my crying. I'd been crying quite often in the last eight months or so.

Samuel said he could tell just from watching this old black-and-white video that Lawrence was a very caring man. I told them that I was quite certain that it was my mother who had insisted that the only way she and Lawrence could reconcile and stay married would be if he cut off all communication with his former girlfriend and their child. And so (to the best of my knowledge) he did.

In that 1951 letter to Rolf's mother Gretchen, Daddy wrote "she is not with me now" in referencing my mother. And his message to Gretchen was "I am writing you to see if you will send me a picture of the boy. And if you want me to send him something, write me and tell me what he needs. And I will send it."

Samuel had written in one of his emails, "*I think that one reason he has no idea about his father is that my grandmother never wanted him to ask about his father. I guess she was emancipated and too haughty to ask for help and wanted to educate his son on her own. Lawrence asked in his letter if she needs anything. Berlin after WWII was totally destroyed and i believe that she needed a lot but wouldn't have ever asked for it."* From what Samuel had heard from his father, there was never anything received by Rolf from his American father, no communication or gifts or money. So my guess is that Gretchen never requested anything, and/or my dad and my mom reconciled, and Daddy agreed to never reach out to Gretchen and Rolf again.

Our plan for the next day was for the four of us to go out to breakfast, but Samuel called me early the next morning and said that Marla was sick. She had been up in the night with a stomach problem and didn't feel like leaving the room, much less eating breakfast out. So they would stay at their room for the morning, and Samuel would have breakfast there in the hotel lobby and take advantage of the pancake machine one more time.

Eric and I had breakfast at home, and worried about what would happen if Marla felt too sick to travel to New York City by bus later that afternoon. Check-out time at the hotel was 11:00 a.m., and so a few minutes before that time, Eric and I drove over to see how she was feeling. They had both packed their suitcases, to prepare to check out, but Marla was still laying down with the shades pulled. Obviously, she didn't feel much better yet. But the couple decided they would still stick with their plan of leaving the hotel, hanging out at our home for a couple of hours, and then we'd still drive them to the bus station at the appointed time so they could head to New York City. Marla thought she felt well enough to handle that.

We brought them to our house and she laid down on our couch, while Samuel asked if he could look through the photo albums some more. I washed dishes and Eric played on his computer downstairs, leaving the young couple alone, and keeping the house as quiet as possible so Marla could nap if she wanted. She did, and after she woke up she said she felt a bit better. While she only drank water, she felt ready at the appointed time to go to the bus station as planned.

We took the highway to get there so the ride would be as smooth as possible for her. We parked the car in the bus station parking lot, helped them unload their suitcases, and get checked in at the ticket counter. While Marla visited the restroom, Samuel, Eric and I were chatting in the waiting area when a manager of the bus terminal came up to Eric and said hello to him.

As it turned out, he and Eric had worked together many years ago in a local manufacturing plant, and he had been our bus driver on one of our trips back from the airport after a vacation several years ago where the two men had chatted and caught up. Eric introduced Samuel to the man and said he was a relative of mine, taking the bus with his girlfriend to New York City to fly home to Germany. Eric mentioned that Samuel's girlfriend was in the restroom and wasn't feeling very well and asked if there was anything that could be done to help her bus trip be more comfortable. The bus manager said there was a particular row of seats on that bus which was more conducive to sprawling out a bit, so he took Samuel's backpack and entered the still-empty bus and placed the backpack on that row to save it for her. Samuel thanked the man just as Marla was rejoining us in the waiting area.

Eric introduced the man to Marla, to which he replied "I hear you're not feeling well. What's the matter honey, are you pregnant?" My eyes widened at this question, and I heard Samuel softly say under his breath "I sure hope not!" while the man laughed loudly, and Eric just shook his head and chuckled.

A few minutes later it was time for them to board their bus, and we gave big hugs all around. It had been a very successful first meeting, and the best part was that Eric and I were planning to see them again in less than a year, this time on their turf. But it was still sad for all of us to say good-bye, especially for me. Even Eric shed a tear as the two waived good-bye to us from the bus doorway. "Those are two really nice young people" he said to me, reaching for his handkerchief.

CHAPTER 16

Planning Our Visit

Based on the successful Skype call with the whole family at Christmas, and the great visit from Samuel and his girlfriend in January, Eric agreed that it made sense for us to go to Germany to meet the whole family in person and spend some time visiting and getting to know each of them. I was very pleased that Eric was now supportive of me in this goal.

A work colleague told me about a travel agency she had used in the past which she found to be very good, so I scheduled an appointment for Eric and me to go there to start making our trip plans. Before the day of our appointment, I emailed Samuel to ask him to check with his dad to make sure us visiting there for Christmas and New Year's was acceptable to everyone. Since Samuel had told me that the entire family rarely all gathers together except for Christmas, it seemed to me that being there during their usual time to all be together would be the most convenient. I didn't want to travel all that way and then not get to meet each of my new family members. But Samuel assured me that arriving a few days before Christmas and then leaving right after New Year's would be fine with all of them.

Both Eric and I were disappointed when the travel agent informed us that all flights to Europe were overnight flights, unless we chose to fly into England. We just wanted a direct flight between Boston and Germany. Neither of us were night owls, so we would have preferred to travel during the day. I was pretty sure that I would be much too excited to sleep during the flight there and would be exhausted after being up all day and all night.

But we decided to bite the bullet and fly at night into Frankfurt. Then we would need to take a short connecting flight to Dusseldorf, and Samuel would pick us up at that airport. For the trip back, we would fly from Dusseldorf to Munich and then back to Boston.

Now that our plans were coming into shape and becoming more definite, I really felt compelled to put forth greater effort to learn to speak and understand German. By now I was getting to the point where I could remember some useful phrases. But it was still very challenging for me. When I would have my half-hour real-time dialogues with a few other students and a native German speaker, I would sometimes find myself slipping a French word into a sentence when I did not know that German word but could remember the word from my high school days studying French. The teacher would chuckle and remind me of the German word I couldn't remember.

While these half-hour guided conversations with other students and the teacher were helpful, the requirement was that the conversations be all in German. So there was no opportunity for any of the students to ask questions in English about the German language, like why sometimes the negative would be nicht and other times it would be kein, for example.

Marla's friend Nora was still working as an au pair near Boston, as her work period had been extended, much to her delight. I still had her phone number from when she had brought Samuel and Marla to visit us, and I had been able to text her a couple of times. She graciously agreed to Skype with me to try to help answer some of the questions I had about the German language and my trying to speak German.

On the day of our video chat, she did her best to answer my questions, and then she asked me if there was anything special I wanted to be able to say in German. I told her that actually, yes, there was. I wanted to be able to tell my brother that I was very sorry that my mother had prevented him from knowing our father. Nora asked me some clarifying questions and then told me how that would be said, slowly enough so that I could write it down phonetically. Then I would be able to practice it on my own over the coming months. It was a pretty long and complicated sentence, and I told her I very much appreciated her help with this. Should the opportunity present itself during our visit, I wanted to be able to express this apology to my brother.

In thinking about how Eric would be meeting my brother for the first time, and reflecting back on other instances of introducing Eric to my various family members when we were first getting serious, I realized another coincidence. When I first brought Eric to my childhood home in Carterville to meet my parents, my dad was sixty-nine years old. And now when we would meet my brother, he too would be sixty-nine.

I mentioned this to Eric and he reminded me of when his parents met my parents shortly after we were engaged. In Eric's and my prior discussions with our parents, they all knew that each of our fathers had served in Europe during WWII. So when we six went out to lunch together so that our parents could meet, Eric's father latched on to that fact, and tried to ask my dad some questions about his time in the service. Discussing this commonality seemed like an obvious conversation topic to both Eric and his father.

But my dad kept deflecting those questions, providing short answers and then trying to change the subject. This proved to be challenging for him because Eric's father was persistent with his questions, and Eric's mom was very quiet. English was not her native language. Canadian French was the primary language in their household while Eric was growing up. Eric learned English in school, and his father learned it through work and his military experience. But Eric's mother was quite self-conscious about her English-speaking skills when she was around strangers. Thus our "get-to-know-each-other lunch" went OK, but without quite as much sharing of information as some participants had desired.

To help our knowledge of how World War II came about, Eric and I enrolled in a twelve-week course through my employer about the history of WWII. Our instructor used a lot of film clips, and we merely audited the course so we didn't have to write the papers other students were assigned. We just read the textbook and supplemental readings and watched the videos. Each student did a presentation at the end of the course on a particular topic of interest to them.

I decided to present last, and only spoke at all because there was a bit of time available. I read a passage from my Uncle Willie's diary which he had kept while he was a German POW. He had been in the Army Air Corps and his plane was shot down over enemy territory. He traded his cigarette rations to his fellow prisoners for their empty matchbooks and used those matchbooks, along with a stub of a pencil he had successfully hidden from his captors, to write about his experiences. The current military and veteran students in the class were particularly interested to hear a little from his writings. Thinking more and more about my Uncle Willie's time in the service, I knew that I would soon need to inform my mom's side of the family about my incredible news.

CHAPTER 17

Telling My Mother's Relatives

When I was growing up, my mother's immediate family would all gather to celebrate Christmas Day every year, first at my grandparents' house, then at my Uncle Willie's, and more recently at my cousin Deb's house. After my mom died, I continued to enjoy spending Christmas afternoon with her side of the family. Therefore, I knew that I would not be able to indefinitely keep the secret of my newly-discovered German family from my mom's close relatives.

Because Deb seemed like the most laid-back and accepting of my mom's family members, I decided to tell her first. Plus, it was only polite to let the hostess know why Eric and I would not attend her Christmas celebration that coming December.

The Rollins side of the family all loved their Uncle Lawrence very much, and his war-time indiscretion was just water under the bridge to them. And they were happy for me that I now have a brother and nieces and nephews. But I wasn't sure how my mother's side of the family would react. My mom's mother was a very pious, judgmental woman, and I could tell from a very young age that Gramma didn't think too highly of my father, although I never could figure out why. Now that I knew of my father's affair, I'm certain that this was the reason for my grandmother's dislike of my dad. And I'm sure she would have expected me to take my mom's side and not acknowledge my brother and his offspring. I didn't think that any of her other grandchildren would have this same attitude, but I wasn't quite sure.

It was now May 2015, just over a year since I learned about my brother. My cousin Deb and her eldest daughter had recently traveled to Italy, from what I had seen on Facebook. I reached out to Deb after she returned, to have a gab-fest and see photos of her adventures in Europe and catch up on things. It was quite unusual for Deb and me to see each other outside of Christmas Day, unless it was at a family funeral. Deb agreed, but I think she knew I had an ulterior motive for getting together. It was unlikely that I would make the hour-and-a-half drive to her home just to see some photos of her recent trip.

I got to Deb and Joel's house, and after she described their trip and showed me a dozen or so photos she and her daughter had taken, it became obvious that I had something on my mind to discuss with her. Her husband Joel made himself scarce, although he was just in the next room. I wondered if Deb may have had the concern that I suddenly wanted some item that had once belonged to our grandmother but she had inherited when her Dad (my Uncle Willie) passed away. Joel stayed within earshot, perhaps as Deb's back-up in case we got into a disagreement.

I knew I had to present her with my story, but I was trepidatious about how she would react. Would she be horrified that her Aunt Rose had been cheated on, and tell me that I shouldn't have anything to do with these people? Or that I was dishonoring my mother's memory? That was my fear; that her reaction would be similar to what our grandmother's would have been if she'd been alive. My hands were cold and clammy as I sat on the couch, and I was happy to have one of the cats jump up near me so that I could pet him. It helped my nervous fingers have something to do. I took a deep breath then exhaled it, as I focused my eyes on my knees and the cat. I looked up at Deb and began the story, rather haltingly, while searching my brain for each word of the script that I had been practicing in my mind each night.

"So, our grandmother… was a rather… opinionated… individual…"

Immediately Deb responded "Ya think?!?"

I smiled at her immediate agreement with me, then continued, "And if there was something… or someone… that she was not pleased with… she really didn't do a whole lot to hide her… displeasure with them."

Deb's face was quite expressionless – I wasn't telling her anything that she didn't already know. So I went on.

"And I always wondered why Gramma was so… displeased… with my father."

"Well, I never noticed any—" Deb began to say, but then stopped herself from finishing the sentence so that I could continue my story.

"I mean, I knew that my parents eloped when my mother was only eighteen, and Gramma might have felt Lawrence 'stole' her little girl at the tender young age of eighteen; and Gramma was very religious, while Daddy was never very religious, and so that was a bone of contention between them." Deb was silent, and I rattled on.

"And Lawrence never was terribly ambitious, to try to make a lot of money to support his family."

Deb seemed to squirm a bit in her seat, like I was "downing" my father and it made her uncomfortable to hear me speak about him this way, even though my tone wasn't critical of him. I continued.

"But I never could come up with any reason why Gramma so disliked my father. But then, a little over a year ago, I learned the real reason why Gramma was displeased with Daddy."

"What was it?" Deb asked, her expression showing some concern as to what I was about to reveal, and whether she really wanted to know about this secret or not.

Once again, I drew in a deep breath and then deeply exhaled. I couldn't stop now. The words slowly escaped from my lips.

"When my father was overseas… serving in Europe during World War II… he was stationed in Germany after the war was over… helping with the reconstruction of that country." My voice then changed to a more judgmental tone, to indicate that I was describing something a bit naughty: "And even though he was married to my mother at the time… he had a relationship with a German woman… and he fathered a child."

I paused to catch my breath, and before I could even have a chance to read Deb's facial expression Joel's voice came booming from the other room, "I'm sorry, I don't think I heard you correctly— did you say he *fathered a child* ?"

I laughed at the surprise of this unexpected listener's comment, and called out to Joel, "Yes Joel, come on in so that you can hear everything better."

Joel stepped through the doorway and stood at the end of the sofa, staring at me with a confused look on his face. At this point, I had to get up from my seat and walk back into the kitchen to grab my folder of photos and documents that I had brought to share with them. I practically ran to get the folder, as I was so excited to share my story with people who seemed receptive to it, and so far, my mother's niece and her husband seemed very interested and receptive.

I brought out the very old, framed photo of my father in his military uniform, taken when he first went into the army in 1943. I laid it out on the coffee table for Joel and Deb to see, and then I pulled out Daddy's military forms, enclosed in a plastic liner for protection. It listed the dates of his service, and Joel was interested to look at this old document while Deb looked at the photo. I continued on about how Daddy was discharged from the army in May of 1946, but the baby wasn't born until November 1946, so my father never got to see his baby son, or hold his baby son, or know his son growing up. When I said this, Joel made a sorrowful sigh, to indicate that he felt badly for my dad.

I continued on, "But he knew *about* the boy's existence… and *my mother* knew about the boy's existence. And evidently, she was *adamant* that I never learn of this 'horrible, scandalous secret.'"

At this point, Deb said, "Oh poor Aunt Rose! She must have felt so betrayed."

It seemed to me that my cousin Deb was feeling more empathy for my mom/her aunt, while her husband Joel was feeling more empathy for my dad. I could relate to both of these feelings, as I had experienced them myself at different times in the last year. I resumed my story.

"My dad never told me that he had a son, even when he was in his last few days on this earth, battling cancer. My mother never told me I had a brother, and she had a decade of living in the house after Daddy passed on. So if there were any hidden items in the house that I could have come across to tell me of this secret, Ma had plenty of time to dispose of them."

"So how did you find out?" Joel asked me.

I told them I had received an email at work, and I brought out the printouts of my email exchanges with Samuel, and the scanned copy of the letter my dad had written to his girlfriend Gretchen in 1951. Then I showed them the photos of my brother, and they too were stunned at the resemblance between Rolf and my father. They were taking in all of this information and working to digest it.

I explained that according to my nephew, my brother didn't speak much English, so I was learning German. I then told them that Eric and I would not be able to spend Christmas with all of them this year, because we would be spending Christmas and New Year's in Germany with my brother and his family. Deb and Joel cheered to hear this news.

"This is so f—in cool!" Joel exclaimed.

They were both thrilled for me and could see how excited I was. My nervousness of the prior days about their reactions had been wasted energy. I asked Deb, "If I had told you about this over the phone, would you have believed me?"

She responded, "Probably not." Thus, she now understood why I needed to visit them to share this information and show them the photos and documents. She said her brothers should have been present to hear it as well, but I told her that I was nervous about telling any of my mother's side of the family, and I wasn't sure how they would react. I thought she and Joel would be OK with it, but I wasn't certain even about that. I said I was fine with them passing along this news to Deb's two brothers, and her children and grandchildren.

I explained how, at first, I was furious with my dad for having cheated on my mother and about how difficult this situation must have been for her. But then after a couple of weeks I felt sorry for my dad, never being able to connect with his son, and I got angry with my mother for preventing them from having a relationship.

Deb said that she felt quite certain that *her* parents never could have known about this.

I said that Eric and I thought they did know. I related the tale about my dad's abrupt change of mood at Deb's daughter's wedding when Eric mentioned to him that one of the young female guests was pregnant. Eric and I felt this was an indication that Deb's parents (father, at least) *did* know.

She responded, "Oh no, that couldn't be, because they always spoke so highly of your dad, and if they had known this secret, they wouldn't have had such good feelings toward him."

I was very pleased that this meeting with my cousin and her husband had gone so well. Since Deb and her husband had been happy about me getting to know my newly found family members, I hoped the other members of my mother's family would feel the same.

A couple of weeks later, I decided to share my news with my mother's first cousin Gwendolyn, who was born just a few years after my mother, and her daughter Rhonda, who was my age.

I usually visited Gwendolyn a couple of times per year, as she was elderly and was in frail health by this point. But her mind was still sharp, and during our visits she would sometimes relate some tale from the family's history, usually involving her father and my grandfather, who were brothers.

Rhonda had a crafts fair at her home every fall, which I liked to visit to find some unique Christmas gifts, and I would include a visit to Gwendolyn's home nearby on my Christmas shopping trips to Rhonda's. I messaged Rhonda and asked if we could schedule a time for me to visit with both her and her mom on a weekend soon, as I had some news to tell them. On the appointed day and time, I arrived at Gwendolyn's home and Rhonda was already there awaiting my arrival.

"What's your big news?" Rhonda asked me after we all sat down in the living room.

I spelled out what I had learned, just as I had with Deb and Joel a couple of weeks earlier.

As I showed them the photos of my dad and my brother, Rhonda exclaimed "So your news is that you have a *brother*?!"

I told her yes, and they could see how happy and excited I was about all of this. Rhonda asked her mother if she had any inkling about any of this.

Gwendolyn responded, "No." She said she would have been in nursing school and/or busy with her work as a new RN during this time.

After I finished all of my description, I told them how Eric and I would be spending our holidays this year in Germany with my new family.

Gwendolyn looked at me and smiled and said, "I'm very happy for you dear. But I'm also glad that your mother is not here to see this."

I could tell that Gwendolyn was feeling sympathy for what her dear cousin Rose must have gone through, which didn't surprise me at all. But I was glad that Gwendolyn was happy for me and not judgmental that I wanted very much to connect with my new family.

CHAPTER 18

Preparing For Our Trip

Six months before our departure date to Germany, I submitted my request for two weeks of vacation time. Because my boss had been so moved by my story, I felt confident I wouldn't have trouble getting this time off, even though *his* boss was now someone new. As it turned out, his tune had changed. I can surmise that his new boss was pushing back on staff taking much holiday vacation time, even though I was submitting my request well in advance. I got frustrated when he emailed me his response that he would "see what he could do" about getting my time off request approved. It appeared that my boss was no longer supportive of my need to meet my brother and other members of my new family. I was on pins and needles for a couple of weeks waiting for an email of approval, and once it came, I saved it. I didn't want anything undermining my ability to make that trip.

I continued to get up early several days per week to work on my German language lessons. By this time numbers (counting to 100), the days of the week, the basic colors, some basic weather terms, a few family terms like *sister, brother, mother, father, son, daughter,* and *cousin,* and a couple of verbs, were well ingrained in my head. I continued to plug away at it, and when trying to speak in the present tense, I did OK. As I got to past tense, it became more challenging. I hoped that the common phrases and sentences that were repeated many times during the lessons would be enough for me to communicate at least somewhat with my brother and little grandniece.

During the spring, summer, and fall months, I happily purchased birthday and anniversary cards for my new relatives, trying to choose the most appropriate card available for each person/couple. And I kept an eye out for ideas for Christmas presents for each person as well. My grand-niece would be turning four years old just a couple of days after Christmas, so for her I wanted to purchase both Christmas and birthday gifts. Finding something that I thought she would like, did not require English language ability, was not overly expensive, and would not be very heavy or take up much room in my suitcase narrowed down the options quite a bit.

I found a large supply of Maine-themed inexpensive T-shirts in my local drug store, and purchased a dozen in various sizes, one for each adult member of the family (there were no children's sizes). At the check-out counter, the clerk asked me if I was buying these for a baseball team or something, and I smiled and said no, for family members in another country. Since the maple glazed nuts had been enjoyed last Christmas when we Skyped, I got another dozen packages at the local farmers market once again, to pair with the T-shirts. I had messaged my niece Christina to inquire what her daughter Sonja liked, and her response was "Winni Poo" which I knew meant Winnie the Pooh. So I ordered a child's T-shirt with Winnie the Pooh on it, in the size I believed was correct given Christina's message to me in metric.

As I came across shiny new 2015 pennies, I put them aside, and planned to pass them on somehow to the little girl during our trip. I also found a kite that looked like a colorful bird and got that for her birthday. At a craft fair I found a very soft throw blanket with a bunny head sewed on at one end. And at the same drug store as the T-shirts I located a travel-sized Etch-a-Sketch, which I thought might be a quiet amusing toy for the little girl. I also got her a stuffed birthday bear and some hand-knitted mittens and hoped that these would be adequate for her Christmas and birthday celebrations.

A college friend of mine originally from Italy, Angelina, was now living in Vienna, Austria with her husband and their daughter. Years before, she had invited me and my roommate Sally to visit her when she graduated from college and went home to Italy. Sally had been able to accept her invitation, but I needed to purchase a car for getting to and from my student teaching assignment the following year. And this same vehicle would be needed for me to commute to a job once I graduated. I could not afford to purchase a car and go to Italy. But now since Eric and I would be fairly close to where Angelina was living, I wondered if we might meet up. I reached out to Angelina and let her know that I had a new family in Germany, and we planned to go to Germany to meet them and get to know each other. Since Cologne and Vienna are relatively close, I wondered if she might be interested in meeting up during our trip. She answered affirmatively and seemed excited to see me again and meet my husband.

At this point, my cousins on both sides of my family knew about my Germany family. Eric had a cousin in town whom he felt a closer connection to than most of the rest of his family now. She and her husband had invited us to spend the last few Thanksgivings at their home, with their extended family, which we enjoyed. I very much appreciated it because I didn't have to cook (I just made and brought my usual pumpkin turtle pie) and I could spend this holiday with family on my husband's side, so there wasn't a continuous reminder that my mom had passed away and was not with us.

About a month before Thanksgiving, Eric and I went out to eat with this couple and I told them about learning of my new family in Germany. They were very surprised and happy for me, as well as happy for Eric that he had the opportunity to travel to Germany as part of my new adventure. We told them we expected to be leaving a few days before Christmas, so we still looked forward to spending Thanksgiving with them, and hopefully do their annual early-December "Yankee Swap" also.

So far, everyone I had told about my new family situation had been very supportive and happy for me. Those among the "Greatest Generation," who I felt were the most likely to have an issue with my acceptance of these family members, were becoming fewer and fewer in number. And as they were cousins of my dad and mom, I had less of a connection to most of them. I was grateful that not a single one of the people I had told gave me grief about it, as I had feared.

CHAPTER 19

Our Trip To Germany: The First Days

As the date of our trip departure neared, my excitement grew. I played over in my mind potential scenarios of meeting my brother for the first time. Even though my imagined scenario of first seeing my sibling on Skype a year before had not played out as I had imagined, I still couldn't help but think about how our first face-to-face meeting would go.

Because late December and early January can be brutally cold in Northern New England, and Nor'easter storms can sometimes knock out our power, Eric insisted that we have our water shut off while we were away. Our flight wasn't scheduled to leave Logan airport until just after 4 p.m. but we knew we should arrive at the airport at least two hours prior to our international flight. And we needed to allow a couple of hours of travel time to get to the airport and match the bus schedule. So I had hoped the plumber would show up to turn off our water in the mid-to-late morning, between his appointments. This would give Eric and I plenty of time to finish packing. But evidently the plumber wanted to get our quick job over with before he got involved in a lengthy job elsewhere, and he drove into our driveway at 8 a.m. Naturally after he was finished, we needed to leave our house so we quickly finished packing and headed to the bus station much earlier than we had planned.

We decided it would be more comfortable hanging out in the airport to wait, rather than the bus terminal. Hence, we were on the 9:00 a.m. bus heading to Boston. When we arrived at Logan Airport, we learned the Frankfurt airport's computer system had gone down for two hours earlier in the day. Consequently, the plane was delayed in leaving Frankfurt, and arrived in Boston significantly later than expected. There was absolutely nothing that we could do except sit in the international terminal and wait for the aircraft and be prepared to board when it was our turn to do so. Needless to say, our day of waiting to fly to Germany was very long.

The flight was crowded – so crowded in fact that when many of the passengers started arriving at the international terminal, one of the crew came over the intercom to let us know that the flight was overbooked, and they were seeking volunteers to take a later flight. There was no way that I was going to volunteer to wait longer to meet my brother. And if they told us we'd have to be bumped, I was prepared to pitch a fit.

But luckily, we were not disrupted, other than our plane being late. Eric and I were not seated together, but we were near enough that we could reach out and touch the other when we wanted to say something. And by each being on the aisle we could stand up and stretch without forcing others to move. The man who sat next to me was very quiet and spent much of the flight trying to sleep. I was much too excited to sleep, but I was not able to read on the flight. Eric seemed to be able to catch a few winks but wasn't very comfortable in the crowded conditions.

I feverishly hoped that we would not miss our connecting flight to Dusseldorf. I did not want to make my nephew and my brother wait for us. And I myself did not want to wait even longer to see them.

We finally arrived at the Frankfurt airport, and then had to go through customs. Because of the delayed flight, I was hoping the line would move quickly so that Eric and I could catch our connecting flight. But there were many people ahead of us in the line, and it seemed to take forever for each person to get processed. Eric and I watched as one stern-looking customs agent grilled a teenage girl, and Eric mentioned to me that this agent reminded him of the Gestapo that he had seen in documentaries about WWII on the History channel.

"I hope we don't get him." Eric whispered. When it was our turn, sure enough, we got that stern-looking agent. He asked where our final destination was, and we told him, and then he questioned why we were going *from* Frankfurt *to* this small city, as Americans are usually going *from* there *to* Frankfurt. I told him that my brother and his family live there, and we planned to spend Christmas and New Year's with them.

And then Eric piped up that my family said they would take us to see the Nürburgring race track and he was very excited to see that. The agent inquired if there were races happening there during our visit, and Eric responded that there were not, but he was still anxious to see the racetrack even in the quiet of December. The agent who had appeared to be scary when grilling the teenaged girl seemed almost friendly toward us after he listened to our story. He finally let us through and directed us to where our connecting flight would be.

We had to go down a very long hallway, and because we were already so late I walked very quickly. Eric, on the other hand, was dead tired after the long flight and the wait at customs, and I had to encourage him to hurry up so we didn't miss our flight. I was still full of energy and adrenaline, knowing that in less than a couple of hours I would meet my brother for the first time.

I was very relieved to get on that plane to Dusseldorf. It was only about an hour or so for this flight, so in no time at all we were *finally* able to end our time in the air. We located the baggage carousel and collected our checked bags. Then we saw two different signs for exiting, one of which was being guarded by two uniformed guards.

We weren't sure which exit to take, and so I asked one of the guards (in English) where we would exit in order to get to the street. He asked me, "Which street?" And I explained that my nephew was supposed to pick us up and take us to my brother's home, and the guard pointed to the other exit and told us to go up one flight of stairs. We climbed the steps of the darkened staircase, struggling with our bulky luggage. The wee hours of the morning (our bodies' time) and my exhaustion were beginning to affect me, and had already affected Eric, as he was tired and getting really frustrated with this whole day and night of traveling.

As I climbed the last few steps, tired from lack of sleep and winded from hauling the weight of my luggage, I thought to myself, *What in the world was I thinking, scheduling my first meeting with my brother for 2:00 in the morning!?*

We reached the top of the stairs and saw the daylight, since it was about 8 a.m. there. As I exited the airport building and began to look around, I heard Samuel's voice call out, "There they are."

I looked up and saw my nephew getting out of a parked car on the street, on the other side of a waist-high wall. First, I saw him standing near the vehicle's passenger side, and then I saw my brother exit from the driver's side of the car.

As he stood up he turned toward us and smiled, and I immediately got tears in my eyes as he was the spitting image of Daddy. I had stared at his photos for many hours over the last year and a half, so I anticipated seeing the resemblance to my dad. But Eric was struck by how much this man looked like his now-deceased father-in-law.

"Wow, he looks like Lawrence." Eric said to me.

I immediately responded, "Well whatever you do, don't call him that."

It seemed to take forever to make our way to where my brother stood waiting for us. While I was very glad to see my nephew again, I was absolutely thrilled to finally see and hug my brother, after anxiously awaiting this moment for twenty months.

To my surprise, I did not break down in tears as I had feared I might do. I merely got borderline weepy, tears welling up in my eyes. Perhaps this was due to my exhaustion, as my body was telling me "It's after two in the morning – go to sleep." Or perhaps this was because Eric had told me a half-hour earlier while we were landing in Dusseldorf to "hold it together" and "not make a scene." Perhaps it was because the moment of our meeting was less perfect than I had imagined – I was dead tired, and it was a bit awkward trying to hug my brother with my big purse over my shoulder and one hand on my suitcase. But I hugged him as best I could and said to him, as I had practiced, "Nett dich kennenzulernen," which means "nice to meet you."

While Eric was struck by how much Rolf resembled Lawrence, I had expected it. But what I had not really expected was the combined joy and pain in my heart when I first laid eyes on my brother, as it was just like I was seeing my wonderful father again, after eighteen years since his death. Naturally I knew that this man whom I had just hugged was *not* my father. We did not even speak the same language. But he had an undeniably strong resemblance to my dad, *our* dad, and the incredible joy of being able to look at and stand near and hug this near twin of my dad's, mingled with the sadness of missing my real father, and knowing that this man and our father could never meet, just tightened my chest for a moment.

I pushed back the tears that threatened to spill from my eyes and composed myself. I had been preparing for this moment for the last year and a half, and I wanted to make a good impression on this man. But I was exhausted, and my 2 a.m. brain just could not put together anything nice to say to him in German. I racked my brain for something – anything – that I could remember how to say in German, that would be somewhat appropriate at that instant, and I finally came up with "Es tut mir leid, ich bin müde" (I am sorry, I am tired).

Samuel asked me what the matter was, and I told him (in English) that I had wanted to be able to have a conversation with my brother in German when I met him. But I was too tired for my brain to function, and I couldn't remember any more of my German at that moment. I was frustrated with myself, but Samuel told me not to worry about it, they understood. We got into the back seat of my brother's Volkswagen and Samuel drove us to our hotel. My nephew asked us questions about our trip, and thankfully Eric did most of the responding. I was speechless, probably from a combination of exhaustion and the weird sensation of riding in a vehicle behind this look-alike of my father. I just zoned out and stared at him.

Once at the hotel, Rolf worked with the check-in agent to sort out our room. While Eric and I were alone with Samuel, Eric told him he couldn't get over how much his dad looked like Lawrence. Samuel smiled knowingly, as he and Marla had also experienced seeing the resemblance of his older sister Christina and me when they first met me in person.

Soon Rolf returned with a hotel worker and a key to our room. My German family then left us to sleep, and Samuel said that in a few hours he would return and bring us to Rolf and Seraphina's home for dinner and to visit. We were both exhausted, and very thankful for a chance to sleep for a few hours.

After a good long nap and shower, we met Samuel and his girlfriend Marla in the hotel lobby and they drove us the short distance to my brother's home. We were welcomed by Rolf and his wife with big hugs and smiles, and Eric and I were better able to appreciate our surroundings than we had been earlier in the day.

My sister-in-law, Seraphina, who had a better command of the English language than my brother, showed us around their home. As we walked near the open-sided stairs to get to the second floor, Rolf pointed out the low supporting crossbar under the stairs and he said he and his sons had to take care not to bump into it with their heads. He said it in German, but with him pointing to the bar and then to his head, and making a grimacing expression, we didn't really need Samuel's verbal translation. It was readily apparent that my brother liked to joke. This was a happy revelation for me, another similarity between him and our dad.

We went upstairs and Seraphina showed us the master bedroom and their "extra" room, which they used for storage. Evidently it's not just Americans who often have a "junk room" where extra things are stored. When she brought us back downstairs and into their family room, I noticed a piano and I said, "Oh, you have a piano!" and she told me that her daughter plays it.

She asked if I played, and since my brother was nearby, I was very thankful for the sentence Rosetta Stone had repeated over and over, so that I was able to readily respond, "Wan ich war ein Kind, ich habe der Klavier gesplielt" ("When I was a child, I played the piano"). Then I was able to say the follow up sentence, "Aber jetzt, ich bin nicht gut" ("But now I am not good"). Samuel was following the group to make sure translations were available if needed, and I think he was very surprised at my adequate German response to Seraphina's question.

Their Christmas tree was up and decorated and I went over to admire it. I asked Samuel if he would take a photo of my brother and me in front of the tree. The two men accommodated my request, and I couldn't help but notice that my brother and I were both wearing grey sweaters with blue jeans. We had not planned to dress alike, but as it turned out we had coincidentally done so. We all sat at one end of their long dining table and had some grapes, cheese, thick-sliced meats, and bread; they had gluten-free bread intentionally for me. And later they brought out some gluten-free *Kuchen* (little cakes or loaves such as zucchini bread or banana bread). I thanked them very much for accommodating my dietary restrictions.

We talked, with Samuel translating for us, and I asked my brother what he does on a typical day, as he is semi-retired. He described some of his frequent daily routines, depending on the day. He indicated that each week on the day Seraphina's housekeeper comes to clean, he gets on the subway to Cologne and spends the day window shopping or going out to lunch with friends or visits Samuel. Eric laughed and said that when our cleaning lady comes once per month, he too leaves our house and goes out to breakfast.

Seraphina explained that she worked in an office "doing administration" for the German government. Consequently, Rolf often cooks dinner to have ready for her when she arrives home. In fact, my brother had made the delicious stew that we could smell cooking in the kitchen. This was very different from Daddy, who made his own breakfast each morning of coffee, orange juice, shredded wheat, and toast. But beyond that, he pretty much only knew how to heat up a can of soup on the stove, or make ham and cheese or peanut butter sandwiches.

After our appetizers, Rolf brought out a photo album of the trip to New York City that Rolf and Seraphina and her two daughters, then teenagers, had taken a few years earlier. This was the one and only time Rolf had ever been to the United States. He showed us pictures of the places they had visited in New York City, and with Samuel's help he described a Barbara Streisand concert they had attended for Seraphina's birthday. Evidently the man who sat next to Rolf at the concert assumed Rolf understood English fluently, and proceeded to try to talk with him for quite a while before the music began. Rolf apparently never bothered to explain to the man that he did not speak English very well, and just let the man rattle on and on. We all laughed. I asked him if he liked New York City and his response was yes, very much. I realized that my brother is much more of a city person than me, our dad, or my husband. But since he had grown up in Berlin, this made sense.

Then Rolf asked if we would like to see a photo album of his childhood. I quickly responded "Yes!" I very much wanted to see photos of his childhood and older family members. He showed us pictures of himself as a young boy and as a young man, photos of his mother, and of her parents. He said that his grandfather had been an important influence in his life during his childhood. He also showed us photos of his mother's two sisters, who had acted as surrogate mothers for him after his mom's death.

Evidently these three women had been working in a factory that provided military assistance to the Nazi party's war efforts. From what I understood, it sounded like they had been working in a factory that had been forced to switch over to manufacturing war materials. So when the Allied Forces marched in to Germany, all of those workers were considered to be helping the enemy, and were rounded up and taken to prisoner of war camps.

My brother showed Eric and me several official school photos of him, and with Samuel's assistance he told us that he didn't know why there were so many photos of him in school because he so often skipped school. He said he never liked school and tried to avoid going whenever he could. The similarity of my dad and my brother not liking school was not lost on me.

Rolf described how his mother had to work a lot, and his grandparents and aunts helped to care for him as a child in addition to his daycare. There was one photo of Gretchen and Rolf and her two sisters in the living room of their small apartment, and on the wall behind them was a framed school photo of Rolf. I pointed to it and said to my brother "Dein Foto" ("your photo"). He looked at the photo more closely and laughed and said yes, although he had never noticed that before.

He then showed us a photo of his mother's grave, all covered in flowers shortly after she was buried. Rolf said that he had been in the military when she had died, unfortunately. I did not understand if he had been away in the military for both her death and her burial, or only for her death. But obviously he felt sorrow that he had not been with her for her last days on this earth.

What he told us next shocked both Eric and me; that this photo from his mother's flower-covered grave was all that he had left of his mother's burial place. In Berlin, and in many other cities in Germany, there is so little land area available for burying the dead, that families only get twenty years of time for their purchased cemetery plot. After that, the family either must pay an exorbitant fee to keep their deceased loved one there, or else the government takes the land back and can use it for other purposes. So it has been several decades since my brother has been able to visit his mother's grave, as it no longer exists.

Since he was talking about the past, and there were some melancholy moments during this discussion, I wondered if now might be the time to tell him my statement in German that I had memorized after help from Nora. Would now be a good time for me to tell him that I was sorry my mother had been the barrier between our dad and him? But just then the phone rang, and Seraphina answered it. It was Rolf's eldest child, Christina, asking if my husband Eric and I were up for her and her husband Timothy and their little girl Sonja to come meet us and visit. Susanne passed along the question and I immediately responded affirmatively. I was a bit tired, but very excited to meet Samuel's siblings. Since others were arriving soon, I quickly shelved the idea of making this apologetic statement to my brother at this time.

Just a few minutes later, Christina and her family arrived. Christina and Timothy gave us welcoming hugs, as Sonja clung to her mom. I crouched down to say hello to Sonja, and although she seemed shy around Eric and me as we were strangers, I did ask her, "Wie alt bist du?" which is, "How old are you?".

She held up three fingers and softly responded, "Drei Jahre alt" which is, "Three years old."

And knowing that her birthday was less than a week away, I then asked her, "Und nächste Woche, wie alt bist du?" which is "And next week, how old are you?" (as best I knew how to say it).

Her eyes then lit up and she smiled broadly as she thrust her arm up as high as she could, all four fingers on that hand extended, and she proudly replied, "Vier! Vier Jahre alt!" ("Four! Four years old!")

My heart just soared. I was able to make a connection with my little grandniece. Those many frustrating times during the last eighteen months trying to learn to speak and understand German suddenly all seemed worth it. Otherwise, I would not have been able to elicit such a happy reaction to my question.

Christina and Timothy asked Eric and me some questions to start getting to know us, in somewhat broken English. It was clear that they were not as proficient in English as Samuel and Marla, but certainly were better able to speak English than my brother. And although Christina was much thinner and a bit taller than me, I could see a resemblance as I stood face-to-face with her. All my life people have told me that I look like my mother. But meeting this young woman whom I also resemble, who was not in any way related to my mom, was surreal for me. Never before had I seen any significant resemblance while standing beside my Rollins relatives.

The phone rang again and this time it was my brother's eldest son, Erik, checking to make sure that it was OK if he and his wife Aida came over at this time. Seraphina announced that this couple was now on their way to meet us. I was very happy to be meeting so many of my new relatives so soon. In a few minutes, both my husband Eric and I would get to meet my eldest nephew Erik and his wife. Anyone saying that name this evening would need to specify whether they meant Eric from the U.S.A. or Erik from Germany.

As we sat in the living room with my niece's family getting acquainted, little Sonja was sitting next to me when we heard the doorbell ring. Suddenly I remembered another pertinent sentence from my German lessons. So I quickly turned to look at little Sonja and caught her eye, my eyes wide with feigned surprise, and said to her, "Oh! Da ist jemand an der Tür!" which is "There is someone at the door!" She immediately smiled and replied, "Ja!" ("Yes!") and jumped up to run to the door to see who was there, and "help" Seraphina let them in. Then she happily skipped back to her seat near her mother Christina, having "helped" allow her Uncle Erik and Aunt Aida to enter. Samuel noticed this interaction and later told me how nice it was that I was able to connect with the little girl in her language. And of course I was thrilled that I was able to do this.

Rolf and Seraphina busied themselves in the kitchen preparing the last-minute items for dinner. Erik and Aida hugged us and asked how our trip had gone. It was obvious that Aida was pregnant, so we asked questions about her due date and if the gender was known yet, and so on. She said that it would be a girl, due in March.

My nephew Erik asked me if what we had seen of Germany so far seemed much different from our home, and my initial reaction was, "Yes, it does seem quite different" which I think surprised him. I think my nephew expected me to say that it really wasn't all that different from what we were used to at home. But what we had seen so far was more suburban, similar to the areas located just outside of Boston, whereas our home was more rural.

Dinner was served, and we all sat down at the long dining table to eat, except for little Sonja who said she wasn't hungry and wanted to just sit on the nearby couch and play with her electronic toy. German potato soup was served, along with sliced meats, bread, and sausages. When I said that the soup tasted very good, Seraphina announced that Rolf had made the soup earlier that day. This then elicited my brother to hold up his index finger which had a plastic bandage on it. He said he had cut his finger while cutting up the potatoes, and jokingly said that whoever found the end of his finger in their soup would win a prize. Eric and I laughed once we heard the translation from Samuel, and looked at each other knowingly. His sense of humor was so similar to Daddy's.

My nephew Erik asked me if I had learned my German language from books, and I told him no, that I had purchased software for my computer so that I could listen to the words and phrases and sentences, and it could listen to my responses. Although I would try to speak to this group in German when I could, my limited knowledge of the language made such instances much fewer in number than my English sentences. To Rolf's credit, there were a few times when I would ask him a question, which one of his children would translate for him, and he would respond with a one- or two-word answer in English. This was a happy revelation for me that he did know some English.

I was so caught up in these incredible moments that I had completely forgotten to capture it through photos. But thankfully my husband Eric thought of it just after we finished eating dinner, and he grabbed the camera to take a few photos of me with my family members around the big table.

I asked my nephew Erik if he too had chosen a year of social service after he finished his schooling, like Samuel had done, and he responded yes. Rolf then said in German that neither of his sons had entered the military like he had done after the end of schooling, and he pretended to shed a tear. Although he was being humorous, my husband Eric and I could sense that Rolf honestly felt some disappointment that neither of his sons had chosen to enter the military. This seemed odd to us, since both young men had chosen careers in fields related to their father's, and their year of social work had been the impetus for this.

I changed the subject and asked Christina's husband Timothy what he did for work. He said that he did auditing and taxes. Erik informed us that in Germany there are more books written about taxes than any other subject, and their tax system is very complicated. Christina spoke up and proudly said that her husband often does her whole family's taxes for them.

Next Samuel informed us that he and Marla planned to take us to the Nürburgring race track the next day, even though it was pretty deserted at this time of year. My husband Eric was thrilled to hear this, being a fan of auto racing. We were both delighted that Samuel would offer to take us to this area, and that everyone we had met was so welcoming.

I was starting to feel a bit weepy at this point, and I didn't want to bring the mood of the group down by crying. And I could see that Eric was starting to get sleepy, even though the time was only about 7:30 p.m. Therefore I asked Samuel if he would mind bringing us back to our hotel as we were getting quite tired from an exhausting couple of days of travel. He and Marla willingly did so, and when they dropped us off, they told us they would come by the hotel in the morning around 9 a.m. to drive us to the racetrack.

Eric and I slowly got ready for bed and talked about the nice evening and interactions with my new family members. So far things were going quite well, and I was so pleased.

CHAPTER 20

Our Trip to Germany: The Days Leading Up to Christmas

When we awoke the next morning, the realization hit me: "I'm in Germany!" I never imagined prior to Spring 2014 that I would ever travel to this country. While I had some vague musings over the years about *maybe* someday visiting France, to see Paris and perhaps the area where my mother's pen pal Simone was from, I never *really* expected to travel to Europe.

Promptly at 9:00 Samuel and Marla arrived to drive us to the Nürburgring racetrack, which was about to close for the holidays. During the somewhat long and rather rainy drive there, we chatted with the young couple about how well things had gone the night before. We also talked with Marla about her father, who had been an engineer for one of the racing teams that regularly competed at the Nürburgring before his recent retirement.

She was very familiar with both the outer areas of the track as well as the inside pits and garage areas, having visited her dad while he worked at some of those races. These areas were not open to the general public during late December, and we felt fortunate that *some* of the track's areas, such as the information center and museum, were open for us to view. Although few other visitors were around, we were able to see the ticket counter area, and the museum area with many old cars and motorcycles on display. They even had life-sized models of famous drivers who had raced on the track, wearing replicas of the fire suits worn at the time of their racing careers. Behind each figure was a large display board covered with their photos and descriptions of their accomplishments. Eric was like a little kid in a candy store. He was thrilled to see everything he could on this visit to the famous track.

Nearby was a large slot car track and a little boy accompanied by his mom was enjoying it, even though he had no competitors. Next there were two racing simulator machines, where visitors could compete against one another in a simulated race on the Nürburgring track. First Marla and Samuel competed in these arcade-type machines, and then Eric and Samuel competed, with Samuel the winner both times.

Then the four of us climbed into the unpadded metal seats of the Motor Mania ride, which took us inside a dark tunnel, and we were to "shoot" only certain items that became visible to us using the "petrol nozzle guns" we each had at our seat. By the time our ride finished, there were more kids using the slot car track, and Eric watched them from nearby. It was a nicely made replica of the roughly thirteen-mile track, although perfectly flat so that the slot cars would readily move throughout the course, whereas the actual Nürburgring course has significant variations in elevation.

We then went into the gift shop, and Eric and I purchased several T-shirts and other souvenirs. I was surprised to see the large clear plastic barrel filled with thousands of ear plugs, in thick layers of pink and green. I had never seen so many earplugs in one spot. We had to walk up quite close to the colorful display to realize that these were merely earplugs.

By the time we were finished taking in all of the indoor displays, the rain had stopped and the clouds were starting to break up. Samuel and Marla then brought us outside and we walked to the section of the grandstands where we were able to see some of the pits and garages. We climbed several flights of stairs and soon were overlooking the row of closed garage doors, below glassed-in suites for spectators who could afford such comfortable seat locations. Eric wanted his photo taken with the garage and pit area behind him, his face beaming.

We took lots of pictures from this vantage point, overlooking the track – many including Eric and me. Eric was still pinching himself that he was actually at this famed spot in racing. By the early afternoon we went back to Samuel's car and headed back toward Lippstadt as we were starting to get hungry. There were many fast-food vendors at the racetrack during the racing season, but now so close to the holidays they were all closed. Before we all got into the car, Marla opened the trunk and handed Eric a couple of books that belonged to her father. He had agreed to loan them to Eric to look at during our stay. While they were written in German, there were a lot of racing photos that Eric was very pleased to be able to see.

On our drive back toward the hotel, Eric and I were surprised to see so much green grass. Back at home, the grass had all turned brown weeks earlier. But here the temperatures stayed more moderate, so their winters were not nearly as harsh as New England's. Samuel drove us to a parking garage near a mall just a short distance from our hotel, and we made our way inside the mall's brightly decorated hallways.

We came to a restaurant and Samuel led us to an empty table. We looked at the menu, which was all in German, except for the "Pommes Frites" or French fries. It looked a bit odd to Eric and me to see some French words mixed in amongst the German menu items. The young couple translated various items for us, and we ordered lunch.

There was a public restroom nearby, accessible from either the restaurant or the mall hallway. But on a counter near the restaurant's seating area were a row of coins. Marla explained to me that those patronizing the restaurant could take a coin, which was necessary to be able to enter the restroom. Those wanting to enter the restroom from the mall's hallway would need to supply their own coin for the turnstile. This was something quite different for me. In my experience, bathrooms have always been freely accessible to those inside shopping malls back at home. I very much appreciated Marla's assistance with this.

Soon the young waiter brought out our food, which included the large order of fries Eric had ordered for the four of us. Eric said they were nearly as good as my homemade ones, and he wanted to return to get some more from this place before the end of our stay.

Samuel told us that the following evening, Christmas Eve, was their usual time for his siblings and him to celebrate Christmas with their mother, Rose, and that this year Eric and I were invited to join them as well. He told us this would be a "traditional German Christmas" celebration. I was thrilled that we were invited for this, and looked forward to joining them, but I also realized I would need to quickly get something other than just the Maine T-shirt for our hostess.

Next we did some window shopping in the brightly-decorated mall, and then took a short walk outside to a nearby Christmas Market. Everywhere there were delicious looking breads and pastries, nuts and candies. Samuel bought a paper bag full of warm roasted nuts with a cinnamon sugar coating, which he said were his favorite thing to get at the Christmas Markets each year. He shared them with us and they were delicious. Then we saw a florist with many plants and flowers for sale, and I decided that the next day Eric and I would return, and I'd get either a plant or a bouquet of flowers to give to Rose.

By this point Eric and I were getting a bit tired, and the kids had some errands to run and would need to get ready to meet some of their friends for a night out. We said our good-byes and Eric offered them his sincere thanks for bringing us to the track. Back at the hotel we rested for a bit, and then I wrapped the Christmas gifts I had packed while Eric looked through the Nürburgring books from Marla's father.

Soon my niece, Christina, messaged me asking if it would be OK for her to come to our hotel room with her daughter Sonja around 10:00 the next morning. I was very excited at this prospect and said that would be great. I wasn't sure what exactly we would be doing with my niece and grandniece for Christmas Eve morning, but I was happy for the chance to find out.

The next morning, Christina and little Sonja arrived at our room. Sonja was once again very shy with us, and she silently clung to her mother. We showed them the view from our room, and I asked Eric to take our picture, the three of us girls. I really wanted a photo of the three generations of Lawrence's similar-looking female offspring. We chatted a little, but the conversation was a bit awkward at first as Christina's English was not as fluent as her younger brothers'.

Then she told us that she needed to buy wrapping paper in preparation for that evening's Christmas celebration with her mother and brothers, and she wondered if we would like to walk to the nearby mall with her and little Sonja. I jumped at this chance to be able to interact more with my grandniece, and to get to know my niece better.

Once we got inside the mall, Sonja's shyness melted away, and she kept walking toward whatever colorful store display or children's play area that caught her attention. She liked saying "Mickey Mouse House" over and over as she walked, which I thought was adorable. We three adults sat on a bench next to one children's play area and talked while my grandniece slid down the little slide, taking turns with other children her age. I asked Christina what she wanted to become as an adult when she was a little girl, and she said a dancer. She had taken dance lessons as a child and had thought that she would grow up to become a professional dancer someday. Before long Christina told Sonja it was time for us to go to the stationery store to purchase the wrapping paper. Christina purchased two large rolls of paper, and Sonja insisted on carrying one of the rolls even though it was longer than she was tall.

Next we headed outside to the Christmas market area so that I could purchase some flowers for our Christmas Eve dinner hostess. On our way to the florist, Sonja spotted a red child-sized convertible car to sit in which was bolted to the flooring beneath, and she immediately ran toward it and got into the seat. Christina tried to call the tot back to the walkway toward the florist, but the child had other ideas. I walked toward the little car, which had a bright white #1 painted on its hood. The girl sat in the car and moved the steering wheel back and forth, and I took her picture, which seemed to please her. She was obviously enjoying pretending to drive the car.

Then she stood up in the seat and pointed to the number on the hood. "Eins" she said out loud, and I responded affirmatively in German, "Ja, Eins." Then I looked at her and said "Eins, zwei, drei," counting to three in German. She repeated back to me "Ja, eins, zwei, drei." I wondered if I could get her to continue and so I said, "Vier" which is four, and then she picked up on my prompt and replied, "Fünf" which is five. It was working. So then I said back to her, "Sechs" which is six and she responded back, "Sieben" which is seven. I was so happy to be able to count back and forth with my little grandniece in her language. It was like a game we were playing, and I wondered how long she would continue to play this with me.

We got up to around twenty before she got out of the toy car, and all the way up to thirty-eight before she decided she was tired of counting, and she scampered back toward her mother and Eric. I was over the moon. I had been able to communicate in a playful interactive way with my little grandniece for several minutes. I was so pleased to have had this opportunity and that my hard work to learn German over the last year and a half had once again paid off. I had a huge smile on my face as I rejoined Eric, and I described to him and my niece what had just occurred. I asked Christina if she would mind if I posted the picture I took of Sonja in the little car on Facebook, and she said that would be fine. So later I shared that photo and description of our interaction, which pleased my closest friends and colleagues to see that our visit was going well.

We then arrived at the florist, and I asked Sonja which color flowers would be best for her grandmother. The child's favorite color was pink so naturally that was the color she suggested. So that's the color I bought to give to Rose in a few hours. By now it was time for Christina and Sonja to head home and do the gift wrapping that was necessary. As we walked away from the shopping area, Eric and Sonja each carried a long tube of gift wrap. Eric started to playfully tap her on the head with one end of the wrapping paper, and then used the tube as a sword and pretended to have a sword fight with little Sonja, which elicited big smiles and laughter from the tot. I was happy to see my husband connecting with my little grandniece also, even though he did not know any of her language.

Soon we arrived at the bus stop and the girls waited for the bus while Eric and I continued to walk back to our hotel. We rested a little bit and then started packing up the batch of presents to bring to Rose Graf's home for that evening's Christmas celebration. As I wrote on the gift tags "To Rose From… " I said to my husband Eric that the last time I had written "To Rose, From…" on a gift tag was when I had wrapped gifts for my father to give to my mother. My dad had not been terribly proficient at gift wrapping, and I had often been tasked to wrap whatever gifts he had purchased for my mom. In addition to doing the wrapping, I had also written "To Rose, From Lawrence" on the tags. This was a nice memory, transporting me back to my teenager days. It made me wistful as we got ourselves ready for the evening of celebration.

We finished packing up the bag of gifts and went down to the lobby to wait for Samuel to pick us up. We waited and waited, and Eric and I started to wonder out loud what was keeping him, as he usually had been very prompt in meeting us. I tried calling him but got a recording that my call could not go through. Just then I received a text from Samuel saying he would arrive in ten minutes.

Soon he drove up to our hotel and was profusely apologetic. He said that in a phone conversation with his older sister a couple of hours earlier, she had told him that she and her husband Timothy would pick us up and bring us to the Christmas celebration. Samuel thought she meant that evening's event at their mom's home. But she meant the next day – Christmas day – to their dad's home. I could tell that Samuel was irritated at this miscommunication and that we were kept waiting. But all was fine. We were just happy to be invited to this Christmas Eve celebration and everyone was well, and that was what mattered.

Just a few minutes later we arrived at Rose's home and Samuel introduced us. She welcomed us with big hugs, and I handed her the bouquet, telling her "Thank you for inviting us to your home for this special evening." Her English was about on par with Christina's and Timothy's, better than my brother's but not as fluent as that of my two nephews Samuel and Erik, who were at their mother's home as well. But their gals, Marla and Aida, were each spending this Christmas Eve with their own families.

Little Sonja showed us into the living room and identified where to place our gifts under her grandmother's lovely fat Christmas tree. There were many lighted candles decorating the room, and the tree was adorned with Christmas lights that also looked like lighted candles. With the primary room lights off, the room had a lovely glow. There were many presents already under the tree, and my nephew Erik helped move some of them to make room for ours.

Then Sonja took my hand and brought us to a little alcove at the foot of the staircase where her "market" was. She had a toy grocery counter, with plastic eggs and fruit and packages of coffee and other grocery items. The little girl was obviously very proud of her market and evidently played with it frequently when she stayed at her grandmother's. Samuel quietly told me that Rose's gift tonight to Sonja would be related to the market, so we would have to "do some more shopping" again later. I thought that this would be the perfect opportunity for me to drop some of the shiny 2015 pennies I had brought with us into her market's change bucket.

Rose and Sonja and Samuel then took us for a tour of Rose's home, ending up back at the living room entrance. Only this time the door to that room was closed. The family had a longstanding tradition of taking photos of the three Graf children outside the room where the Christmas tree stood and gifts would later be opened. Once Rose was satisfied with a couple of nice photos of her three children, then she joined them for a few photos, and next Timothy and Sonja joined in as well. Then Eric and I were included in photos which Timothy took, some with and some without Rose. It was wonderful to be a part of this year's annual family custom.

Once we were all satisfied with the photos, Samuel explained that according to tradition, the youngest member of the family would open the door into the celebration room and would take a small bell off a low branch of the tree and ring it continuously, while Rose put on the CD player to play a German Christmas song about children ringing Christmas bells. Next a couple of additional German Christmas songs were played on the CD, while the others sang along. Then we all sat at the long table which had Christmas table settings and crystal goblets. Rose made a Christmas toast, thanking God for their health and being together, and mentioning being thankful for Samuel finding Eric and me, and bringing us together now with the rest of their family. We each had some *Kuchen* cakes and cookies and beverages, and I took more photos while everyone chatted.

We opened Christmas presents, with each gift giver taking turns going to the tree and picking up the gift to be given. Sonja happily helped by bringing the gift to the correct recipient after being told by the giver who it was. Samuel gave Eric and me a book about Cologne, along with a tourist guide and street map, to assist us with any sightseeing around the city that we might want to do this coming week. Rose gave us a stained-glass manger scene hanging decoration, which replicated one in the Cologne Cathedral's stained-glass windows. Erik and Aida gave me a calendar of pretty German scenes and gave Eric a calendar featuring a German race car driver and his cars. They also gave us a book about scenic places to visit in Germany.

Christina and Timothy gave us a calendar with photos of them and of Sonja, and with drawings Sonja had made. And Sonja gave us a paper house made out of green construction paper with cut out windows, which Rose had helped her make. Inside it was a small plastic battery-operated votive candle, which caused light to shine out of the "windows" and tiny pin pricks in the shape of a tree in one of the paper walls of the house. It was very cute and special to me, and I hoped I would be able to cover it adequately to protect it from being crushed on our trip back home.

I asked if it was OK to break their tradition of handing out gifts one at a time, as there were so many gifts that were identical to several recipients. Rose and Samuel approved, and I handed Sonja her first gift, a royal blue child's T-shirt with Winnie the Pooh on the front of it. Then she helped me distribute the wrapped Maine T-shirts, which were identical except for the sizes. Everyone opened their packages, and then immediately put on their new T-shirts over their other shirts. Sonja saw them doing so and she too put on her Pooh T-shirt over her long-sleeved T-shirt. I was heartened to see them all pleased with their gifts. They all gathered together so that I could take a photo of the whole group wearing their matching T-shirts, each wearing a big smile.

Then I handed Sonja the wrapped hand-knitted mittens, and upon opening them she immediately put those on also. She happily stood for a couple of photos wearing her new T-shirt and mittens. Then Rose handed the child a heavier package, which were winter boots. It was funny to watch the child clomp around her grandmother's warm living room wearing winter boots and mittens.

Next I distributed the New England Patriots-themed paper plates and napkins. Lastly, I handed Sonja a wrapped package of maple glazed pecans to give to her grandmother Rose, who asked me if they had been made in Maine. I told her that most likely the nuts were not grown in Maine, but the maple syrup used to sweeten them had been made in Maine.

After we finished opening the presents, we made our way back to the long table while Rose brought out the food. She set an indoor barbeque grill in the center of the long table, and then placed serving plates of small pieces of pork and chicken and a variety of chopped vegetables, including previously-cooked potatoes cut into wedge pieces, on the table. Each place setting had a heat-resistant paddle, and each person could select what vegetables they wanted to have warmed by the bottom section of the grill (which was indirect heat), while indicating what meat they would like cooked on the top of the grill, with direct heat. So instead of make your own tacos night, like some folks do back at home, this was a cook-your-own-meat-and-vegetables night. Eric and I had never seen such an appliance.

We chatted over the meal about our flight and our experience at the Nürburgring. By this time, little Sonja was busying herself with her little store and getting her brand new cash register set up. I went over and "bought" some of her grocery items, paying for them with the shiny 2015 pennies.

Christina then asked me what I thought when I first received Samuel's initial email. I told her and the others that I thought he was lying and had merely reached out to me to stir up trouble after finding my father's name on the World War II Memorial web site. My husband Eric described how we felt that Samuel's story could not be true, based on our knowledge of Lawrence.

Pretty soon Christina and Timothy decided that it was time to leave and put Sonja to bed, as they were certain she would wake up early Christmas morning. After their family left, Rose brought out dishes of ice cream with a cinnamon toping sprinkled on top. This reminded me of the pumpkin turtle pie that I had served during Samuel's and Marla's visit to us. Then my nephew Erik wanted to leave to go to his in-law's home to spend some of the evening with them and his wife. Samuel told Erik he would drop him off near his in-law's home on the way to bringing us back to our hotel.

During the short drive, my husband Eric told my nephews that in his opinion, they had made the smart choice by choosing to do a year of social work rather than a year in the military after finishing school. And I agreed, since they had each chosen careers related to social work, so this type of profession obviously resonated with them.

I was extremely happy that Christmas Eve with so many of my new family members had gone so well.

CHAPTER 21

Christmas Day

On Christmas Day, all four of my brother's children would be at his home in the evening for their big Graf family Christmas celebration. Most years they all gathered on a day other than the twenty-fifth of December to celebrate the holiday, to allow everyone to spend that day with spouses' family members. But because of our visit, this year was special.

Eric and I had a leisurely morning to ourselves. After breakfast we packed up the remaining Christmas gifts to bring with us for the celebration later. We also packed our shoes to wear that evening. Christina had warned me that we would need to wear sneakers and bring our Christmas celebration shoes with us, as we would be "going for a little walk and to visit a cemetery" first. It was raining quite hard, and we wondered if their outdoor plans would change due to the weather.

Soon my niece, her husband, and my grandniece arrived. Timothy drove us through the rainy, dreary streets to the area where the cemetery was located. To Eric's and my surprise, there were many other vehicles in the parking lot, including some buses full of older people. Evidently there is a tradition in Germany that on Christmas Day, many people go to visit the graves of their deceased relatives. Timothy's mother and grandparents were all buried here, and the number of years he could continue to visit his grandparents' grave was getting short. Though he still had quite a few years left to visit his mother's grave, that, too, would one day come to an end. Obviously, many Germans include visiting graves of recently deceased family as part of their Christmas Day activities.

There was quite a long path for us to traverse in order to get to the appropriate area, with many trees and a few benches lining the sides. It was a beautiful area and would have been even more attractive in sunnier weather. Timothy placed flowers at his mother's grave and we were all silent for several minutes. Then Christina told us how wonderful her mother-in-law had been. She said how sorry she was that Sonja would not be able to really know her paternal grandmother very well, as she was too young to remember much about her. We then walked further along the path to the grave of Timothy's grandparents. Never before had I seen so many people all visiting a cemetery in the pouring rain.

Pretty soon we headed to Christina and Timothy's apartment so that they could get Sonja into some drier clothes. She had done some puddle jumping during our excursion and was quite wet. Once home, the little girl's parents got her changed as Eric and I made ourselves comfortable in their living room, watching their fish swim in the large tank and admiring their Christmas tree. Soon the little girl wanted to take us on a tour of their home, as she had done at her grandmother's. When she showed us her bedroom, her mother Christina asked her where her "American friend doll" was, and Sonja quickly located it. The fact that she knew right where the rag doll was implied to me that she played with it regularly. It made me glad to see that what I had selected for her Christmas gift a year ago was appreciated. Sonja then wanted to show us her toy kitchen, similar to her "market" at her grandmother's house, and her new toy parking garage with small toy vehicles on the various ramps.

Soon we were talking more with Timothy and Christina than paying attention to Sonja's toys, and so she then wanted to show us her photo album of her baby pictures. I was thrilled at the prospect of seeing photos of the little girl and her family. I was particularly interested to see the photos of my brother holding his grandchild. Although there was definitely a difference in the men's ages, the photos of Rolf holding his grandbaby Sonja resembled old photos of my dad holding me as a baby.

Once we finished looking through that photo album, Christina asked if we would like to look at the album of photos from her and Timothy's wedding. I so enjoyed seeing these photos, some of which included a teenaged Samuel. We laughed at how different his hair looked at that time compared to now.

Soon it was time to squeeze back into their car and head over to Rolf and Seraphina's home for the Christmas celebration. When we arrived Seraphina took our coats and our bag of presents, and then introduced us to her mother and to her youngest daughter, Lettie, who were also there for the evening's celebration. Then Samuel and Marla arrived, looking very festive.

Before long, my younger niece, Lorraine, and her boyfriend, Dietrich, arrived. We had met them via the Skype call a year earlier but this was the first time we met them in person. We chatted with them a bit to get to know them more, and shortly thereafter Erik and Aida arrived. With everyone now present we were ready to begin the celebration with German cakes (*Kuchen*) and beverages. We all sat at the long dining table, which had seemed incredibly long on last year's video call. But with Rolf's whole immediate family in attendance, including Seraphina's daughter and mother, as well as Eric and me, that table was comfortably crowded. The room was filled with people's voices and laughter, and I was so happy to be here with my whole German family.

Rolf got up, went to their Christmas tree and brought gifts back to each member of this extended family – a very nice hand cream and body lotion set for each of the women, and men's shower gel/shampoo and cologne set for each of the men. Then one by one, each of the family members handed out their gifts, with little Sonja's help. We received some wooden Christmas ornaments from Seraphina's mother and daughter.

Next Rolf handed me a present and said it was for both Eric and me, from the whole family. I opened it and it was a mounted photo of my whole German family, taken at a castle on a high hill with a beautiful scenic area behind them. My brother, Seraphina, her mother, her daughter, Erik, and Aida had all been there in person, and Lorraine had used her skills with Photoshop to drop into the picture all the other members of the family who had not actually been present when that original photo was taken. So everyone there at the evening's Christmas celebration was included in this ready-to-frame photo. I was very happy to have this and would be sure to pack it carefully for the trip home.

When the others had finished handing out their gifts, I asked Samuel if it was OK if I started handing out our gifts and he said that was fine. With little Sonja's help, I gave out the remaining Maine T-shirts to Aida, Marla, Rolf and Seraphina, and Lorraine and Dietrich. Then Eric helped me hand out the maple glazed pecans to each couple.

Sonja and I handed out the slipper-socks for the women, and the lighthouse-themed socks for the men. Next I gave the soft bunny-headed blanket/throw to Sonja to open, and I handed a T-shirt from my place of employment, the Maine college for adults, to my brother. After he opened it, he evidently chuckled while telling Erik and Seraphina that he was afraid to wear it in public, as people might think he spoke English and try to converse with him.

Then I had Sonja hand Aida a gift for the baby which was due in March. Everyone ooh'd and aah'd at the tiny onesie as Aida held it up. Then I gave Sonja the travel-sized Etch-a-Sketch, which was a strange item to everyone except my husband Eric and me. Sonja played with it for a little bit after I showed her how it worked, and when she tired of it, put it down on the coffee table. Her dad picked it up and started working on it. First he wrote Sonja's name, showed it to me and Sonja, and then he erased it and wrote my name. He was quite adept at it for a first-time user.

Last I handed out the wrapped Carterville postcards to my brother, two nephews and two nieces, each of which had a heartfelt, handwritten message from me, as well as a 2014 and a 2015 penny taped on. As each family member read the message (Samuel had to translate Rolf's for him), I said loudly, "I wanted each of you to have something from Carterville." As I finished my statement, I was overcome with emotion and started to weep, despite trying to hold back the tears. Each of my new family members came over and gave me a hug, one at a time. They all recognized that this was a very emotionally charged day for me, spending Christmas with this whole big family that I never knew I had.

The table was cleared of all the presents and leftover cakes, and several family members started working on finishing the preparations for the Christmas dinner and setting the table. Others were chatting in various areas of the home, away from the noisy kitchen and dining area.

Since a few people were congregating in the room where the piano was located, Eric asked Seraphina if she minded if I played it a little bit. My sister-in-law said no, she didn't mind at all. So I used a couple of fingers to pick out the melody of "99 Luftballons." As I played it, Christina started dancing to it behind me, and Sonja was fascinated to see me playing and her mother dancing. When I finished, everyone clapped, and Samuel told me that the song was Christina's favorite back in the 1980s. This was a very pleasant revelation, to learn that the one German song I could share was a favorite.

Sonja wanted to try playing the piano, so her dad Timothy stayed with her in the room and closed the door, while she fiddled with the keyboard keys as young children like to do. Everyone else started milling about closer to the kitchen, as wine was starting to be poured. Eric and I stood in the hallway next to a print of Rolf's favorite author and talked with Samuel about who it was. As Rolf joined us, he mentioned what a bright little girl Sonja was. Then, smiling slyly with a twinkle in his eye, he said in German that children get their intelligence from their grandfathers. Samuel translated, adding with a smile, "Then it's a good thing that Lawrence was intelligent!"

We chatted more with Samuel and Marla as Rolf headed back to the kitchen, and soon he was calling for everyone to sit down for the meal. Rolf proposed a toast to my husband and me joining them for this occasion, and then folks passed around the plates of food for all to share. There were a variety of sausages, sliced cold cuts and cheeses, breads and a variety of salads including a dark red salad made with cabbage and beets and herring, which was very good. There were lots of conversations occurring around the large table full of people, and plenty of food and drink— overall, it was just a delightful evening.

When the meal was over and people started to clear the table, Dietrich and my nephew Erik headed out onto the balcony to smoke cigarettes. After they returned inside, my husband inquired if Cuban cigars were available in Germany. Rolf overheard this conversation, as the young men responded that they did not know. Rolf asked his son Erik to translate what my husband had asked, and then Rolf looked at Eric and held up one finger, indicating that he wanted my husband to wait a moment. My brother headed upstairs and when he came back down he was holding a metal tube containing one Cuban cigar, which he handed to Eric. Rolf told his son, who translated to us, that a few years ago someone had given Rolf that cigar, but Rolf did not smoke so he was giving it to his brother-in-law as an additional Christmas present. Eric was thrilled, as he had never tried a Cuban cigar before.

Then Rolf had another photo album to show me, and I sat beside him at the table. His hands looked a lot like our father's but without the worn, calloused look of Daddy's. With so many people in the home for hours, it had gotten quite warm, and my brother had taken off the bright red pull-over sweater he had been wearing when we arrived. It wasn't lost on me that his blue long-sleeved shirt exactly matched my royal blue dress, as we sat next to each other and looked at the photos. This was the second time Rolf and I had dressed in the same color clothing.

After we finished looking at the pictures and engaged in some more conversations with my nephew Erik and his wife, I started to get tired. At one point Rolf saw me looking pensive, with no smile on my face, and he asked Samuel to ask me what I was thinking about. He did, and as I could see both men were looking at me for my response, I looked at Rolf and replied, "Du siehst wie ihm," which is "You look like him."

The Days After Christmas

We had a pretty exhausting day on Christmas and were glad to have some time to sleep late the next morning. I was still basking in the glow from the evening's celebration. Although there were some bittersweet moments, it was my best Christmas ever.

After breakfast, we headed out to the park so Eric could smoke his cigar, which he thoroughly enjoyed. Although it was a nice day the park was quite deserted, and we had plenty of space to ourselves to wander about and enjoy the beautiful area.

Later, Erik, Aida, Rolf, and Seraphina brought us to Erik's workplace, a day care center/preschool. It was a new and rather large facility, and Eric and I were very impressed with it from our private tour. Erik and his female colleague were co-leaders of this center, and from what Erik described to us, Rolf had worked for approximately one year to get the funding laws adjusted so that this facility could actually be built in this location. I had learned from our first evening getting to know my brother that he had attended law school and had used this training to supplement his social work background. This beautiful new early childhood learning facility was a source of pride for both my brother and his eldest son.

Then we headed to our next destination, a medieval castle that was now a historical museum and tourist attraction. Evidently much of the original castle had been destroyed but then it was rebuilt in the early 1800s. My nephew, husband, and I each took turns in the stockade with Aida taking photos of us as mementos. There was also a tall statue of a knight in armor sitting on a horse, with the man's date of death listed as 1225. This was the oldest date on a statue that I had ever seen. Next we entered the ground level floor of the castle, and went into the huge function room. There were beautiful stained-glass windows, a long wooden table with red velvet cushioned chairs, and a fireplace at one end of the room. On the opposite wall was a large mural of a battle scene, showing knights with swords and shields, others with bows and quivers of arrows, still others with various medieval weapons, all engaged in battle or running toward the fray.

Then we climbed the stairs to check out the various other rooms. These included a weapons room which was Erik's favorite, a room of helmets, a room with various suits of armor, and a room with musical instruments from that time period. There was also a replica of a bedroom from that time period which included a red housecoat hanging up. At this point Rolf and I were standing next to one another looking in at this room, and I pointed to the house coat. I asked him in German "Ist das dein Hausmantel?" ("Is that your housecoat?"), to which he replied "Nein, meiner ist blau" ("No, mine is blue"). We both chuckled at our little joke together. I was happy to be able to say enough in German to get a smile and chuckle out of my brother.

In one hallway, I took a picture of Eric with his arm around the shoulder of a suit of armor which was short enough for him to reach. We did notice that many of the suits of armor were meant for men much shorter than most of the German men we had met in the last few days.

Then my nephew Erik asked our group who among us wanted to climb up to the crow's nest area, and Eric and I both said we did. Pregnant Aida and both Rolf and Seraphina said they would stay down below and wait for us to complete our adventure. Erik led us up many flights of stairs, some of which were quite steep, and through passageways with snipers' dens along the way. At the very top we were treated to spectacular views of the area. We even saw a wedding taking place on one area of the grounds.

After finishing our tour, we walked down the hill to a Waffle Haus restaurant for some supper. Eric and I were used to waffles being a breakfast food, but the Germans often consider waffles an evening food. Most of us ordered waffles with fruit on them, but my nephew ordered this establishment's popular pizza waffle, which intrigued my husband. After we finished our meal, the sun had set, and Rolf and Seraphina left us with Erik and Aida for the evening. They drove us to an area outside of the city to get a nice view of the twinkling lights in the distance.

Then we headed to a bar to talk some more and get to know each other better. We were feeling very comfortable chatting with the young couple, so I told them of the sentence I had memorized in German that I wanted to tell my brother, about how sorry I was that my mother had prevented him and our dad from knowing each other. While they both said that my memorized sentence was spoken correctly, they were a bit wary of my expressing that sentiment to my brother. I told them that if the family felt that I should *not* say it to Rolf, then I wouldn't. I certainly did not want to cause any sort of consternation.

The next day was little Sonja's fourth birthday, and a family party was planned for mid-afternoon at Christina and Timothy's home. But closer to midday, Rolf, Seraphina, and Erik came by to pick us up for our next adventure. My brother drove us all to the beautiful Japanese gardens on the grounds of Bayer Industries, which I had not realized is a German company. It was a lovely day, not nearly as cold as a typical day in late December in New England. We strolled along the paths and enjoyed the beautiful flowers, trees, fountains, coy ponds, and little waterfalls. It was an absolutely gorgeous park and very relaxing. There was also a Japanese tea house that had been dismantled in Japan and brought to this spot and reassembled. At one point I couldn't help myself and said out loud, "I'm just so struck by the irony that the reason I'm here today, standing in this beautiful *Japanese* garden, in *Germany*, is because we – the U.S.A.– were at war with these two countries seventy years ago!" My husband looked at me like I probably shouldn't have said that, while my nephew looked back at me and nodded.

There were numerous moments during our leisurely stroll when I was suddenly transported through my memories back to being with my dad once again. He loved being outside whenever it was good weather, tinkering on some small engine item like a snow blower or lawn mower (either his or a neighbor's), or even just strolling around the yard smoking a cigarette. When it was chilly enough for his nose to start to run, he'd pull his white cloth handkerchief out of his back pocket, wipe his nose, and then fold it and put it back into his pocket again. He often wore a dark colored quilted jacket and a dark navy flat cap in the spring and fall.

Now at this moment, following along behind my brother who was wearing a dark quilted car coat and a dark rounded "Andy Capp's" style cap, he looked so much like our father. Rolf's clothes were unquestionably much nicer and probably much more expensive than the work jacket I had seen my dad wear for so many seasons, but he still reminded me so much of my memories of Daddy. He'd make a particular hand gesture, and I'd see my dad; he would hold his head a certain way, and I'd see my dad; he'd take his handkerchief out of his back pocket and wipe his nose, fold it nicely and put it back into his pocket, almost like Daddy used to do. I swear that I could feel my dad's presence there with us in that beautiful outdoor area. It was a surreal experience for me.

We got back into the car and went to see where Erik's and Aida's wedding reception was held just a couple of years earlier. We drove to a beautiful art museum building with a lovely courtyard outside. We then headed to Erik and Aida's apartment, where I noticed that they had already put up on display the postcard with my hand-written message and pennies on it. Aida had some coffee brewing and appetizers put out, and we all sat down to have a bite to eat while Erik went to "make himself more comfortable." He exited their bedroom wearing a long-sleeved Boston Bruins shirt.

Then Aida asked if we would like to see their wedding photo album and I was tickled to see it. Aida was a beautiful bride, and Erik looked so handsome in his dark blue suit in their many photos. Then Aida asked if we would like to see their photo album of pictures taken at Rolf and Seraphina's wedding, and I was even more excited to see this album. This wedding looked to have been a bit more low-key, as it was a second marriage for both of them. But it didn't matter to me; I was very happy to be able to see pictures from my brother's wedding. A much-younger Samuel was more blond in these photos, and when Eric saw this he exclaimed, "Here Samuel looks just like Justin Bieber!" which caused us all to laugh heartily.

By then it was about time for us to go to the birthday party. We needed two vehicles for all of us, some folding chairs, and all the gifts. We eventually left behind the busy streets for a quieter neighborhood. Once we parked near the apartment, Erik took the basket of gifts out of the car while Rolf took out the folding chairs. But rather than immediately walk toward our destination, my brother instead set up one folding chair in the middle of the quiet street, sat in it, and with a silly grin on his face began waving to pedestrians on the sidewalk and calling out "Hallo! Hallo!" as he waved. Eric and I watched this, and how pleased Rolf seemed with his little joke, and then we looked at one another knowingly. This antic reminded us of Lawrence to a T. The "nature vs. nurture" debate was settled in both of our minds – there were so many similarities between these two men even though they had never met.

Many of Timothy's family members had already arrived at the celebration, along with Samuel and his mother. I was glad to see my brother, his current wife, and his ex-wife getting along so well together. Sonja was very excited to open her presents and cards, and when she opened the card from us and saw the large number four on the front of it, she happily said "Vier!" Then she opened the stuffed bear that said "Happy Birthday" on its big round belly, and I showed her that when his belly was poked, the "Happy Birthday" song would play. Since we had watched her poke the belly of the rag doll we had given her a year ago on our initial Christmas Skype video chat, I knew that she wouldn't hesitate to poke the bear's belly.

She continued to select gifts out of the basket and soon she came to the bird kite I had selected for her. When I saw this kite in a store many months ago, it had reminded me of the photos Christina had emailed to me of Sonja standing in front of a big wooden bird with outstretched wings, with measurements clearly marked on the wings. At a zoo they sometimes frequent, there was a stump for a child to stand on in front of this "measurement bird," and the child could hold their arms out to see how far they could reach. The first photo I saw of Sonja doing this made me laugh out loud because her two-year-old face indicated by her expression that she was *not* at all happy about this.

The birthday girl still had several more gifts to open, and at this point Rolf and Aida were sitting near me, quietly watching the festivities. Then Rolf told Aida he had a story to tell me but would need her assistance to translate it for me. Aida said she was happy to help. He told us of how when he was a very young boy living in Berlin, his mother worked as a secretary for "a very important man." This would have been in the very late 1940s or around 1950, during the Cold War when Russian influences were strong in that area.

As the child of a single mother, little Rolf had to go to day care while his mother Gretchen went to work at the office each day. One day, for some unknown reason, after little Rolf was dropped off at the day care, he became very agitated and began to scream and call out for his mother non-stop. Nothing the day care workers did would get little Rolf to calm down. It got so bad that they had to telephone his mother to come and get the boy. Evidently something that required Gretchen to be present in the office was happening on that day, and so she did not want to leave her job but felt she had no choice.

Because she left work to take care of her young son, the "very important man" fired her. Another secretary was quickly hired to replace Gretchen. About three weeks later, Gretchen heard that both the "very important man" and his secretary were "taken." They both disappeared and no one ever heard from either of them again. Evidently it was common knowledge of occasional instances of the Russians apprehending - basically kidnapping - people they felt were a threat to the Russian government. It was very fortunate for both my brother and his mother that he had screamed uncontrollably for her on that day, causing her to lose that job.

After enjoying birthday cake, Sonja played with her new witch's broom toy, and her Uncle Samuel would pick her up and help her fly around the room with it. Each lift would elicit a squeal of delight from the child.

Soon it was time to leave. Samuel told me on his way out that he would see us the next evening in Cologne, after we switched from our current hotel to one in Cologne near the cathedral. Timothy stayed at home with Sonja while the rest of us headed to an Italian restaurant. Over pasta we chatted about favorite movies and actors, singers, and favorite foods, and I learned that my brother really enjoyed *The Naked Gun* movies, which did not surprise me.

We had enjoyed another wonderful day together.

CHAPTER 23

December 28 and 29, 2015

The next morning, Eric and I finished packing up the last of our belongings after a big breakfast. Soon Rolf and Christina arrived at our room to help us check out of our hotel, go by train to Cologne, and check in to the hotel where we would stay for the second half of our visit. We each maneuvered one suitcase down to the lobby and then outside toward the train station.

Once we arrived at the Cologne station it was only a short walk to our hotel. I went to the front desk, rather surprised at how elegant the lobby was. Eric and I had not anticipated our hotel being so upscale for the price. The front desk put our luggage in storage for us for the few hours until we could check in, and we headed out to see some of the sights of Cologne, the first one being the huge Cologne Cathedral, or Kölner Dom. I was taken aback by how tall the spires were, how black it looked, and just how massive this church actually was. I was much more used to seeing small white churches at home.

The photos I had seen simply did not capture the enormity of the structure. Its main entrances opened out to many stone steps, with a large plaza at the bottom of the stairs. We looked at the several black and white photos that are on display near the cathedral, showing how the area looked right after the end of WWII when the cathedral was still mostly intact, but the surrounding area devastated. It was very sobering.

Next we wanted to eat, so we decided to tour the cathedral later. We walked to a nearby cafe, Rolf's favorite spot to go on his weekly trips to the city. As we entered, we passed by a very large glass case full of candies, next to a second glass case filled with delicious looking pastries. My brother got us a table while we ogled the confectionary goodies. After eating our lunch Eric was considering ordering a piece of cake for dessert. He decided to try one, and he went to the glass cases and looked over all the various cake options, pointing to which cake he wanted to try.

Soon our waitress brought him his piece, but he took one bite of it and immediately made a horrible face. He groaned and exclaimed, "It's banana!" I said, "Oh no! Of all the different cakes you had to pick from, you chose the one flavor you hate!" My husband decided that was a sign he should not indulge in dessert.

Then we headed off for more sightseeing of the city, starting with the interior of the Cologne Cathedral. Near the entrance Eric overheard two women speaking English with a Southern U.S. accent and he looked at them and said "United States?" and they responded affirmatively. So he struck up a conversation with them and found out they were from Virginia. I guess he was missing being able to readily strike up a conversation with friendly-looking strangers he encountered, as so many of the people here that we spoke to struggled somewhat with speaking English back to us.

We wandered around the huge interior of the church and saw the display of what is claimed to be the location of the bones of the three wise men. Christina and my husband both expressed some doubt about that claim. We looked at the many different stained glass windows, unsuccessfully attempting to locate the one depicting the manger scene, like the reproduction glass plate Rose had given us for Christmas.

When we tired of the dark, damp cathedral's interior, we went into a nearby cigar shop and Eric looked around to see if he could find any more of the cigars like Rolf had given to him. This particular shop had none. Then we went to a souvenir store, and Eric and I each purchased some items depicting the Cologne Cathedral.

At one point during our meandering, Christina asked Eric if he had an accent, because she could not understand him as well as she could me. Eric was surprised to hear that and asked me if I thought he had an accent.

I told him I did think he had a little one, a combination of Northern New England Yankee and French Canadian. So that helped him to understand why Christina and her husband didn't laugh as often at things he said trying to be funny, while Samuel and some of the others did laugh. It wasn't that they didn't have a sense of humor, but that they had a harder time understanding what he was saying.

We then went to the train platform so that Rolf and Christina could show us where to stand to get the correct train in the morning; we were going to Nuremberg to meet up with my college friend Angelina. They showed us where to locate the schedule and how to read it about the outgoing trains. Then he said – in English – "My sister is an intelligent woman; she can find it." I was thrilled to have him call me his sister. And for him to say this in English was just delightful.

By this time, we could check in to our hotel room, and were starting to get weary from being on our feet. So after making sure that our room was OK, my brother and niece bid us goodbye and headed toward the train station to go back to Lippstadt. Eric and I were pleasantly surprised at the large hotel room we had, with a huge bathroom. We rested and unpacked and got settled in to our new "home away from home."

That evening, Samuel, Marla, and Marla's good friend Nora (who was back home from her stint as an au pair in Boston) arrived at our hotel to bring us out for dinner at a restaurant that served "traditional German food." We walked to the train station and took the *U-Bahn* (subway) to a different area of the city. I was happy to have a chance to thank Nora in person for her assistance with helping me last summer to memorize the apology statement in German to my brother, although I wouldn't be telling it to him after all. Samuel said that several members of the family agreed that my apology was probably best left unsaid.

Eric and I tried the *Wienerschnitzel*. The food was delicious and it was a bit of a relief to be spending this time with fluent English speakers, although our communication with my brother and niece earlier in the day had gone better than we had feared. We had a nice relaxing evening and walked back to the subway station.

Once we were back in central Cologne, Samuel asked if we would like to see his flat and we said most definitely. So we walked the short distance to his apartment building and climbed the couple of flights of stairs to his studio apartment. Marla said that these buildings were some of many built shortly after the war, and put up quickly, with thin walls, for the factory workers to live in. These laborers would then quickly get to work making Germany productive again. Samuel said it was small but comfortable for him to live in by himself.

We were surprised to see a poster of Alf on his wall, as up until that moment we did not know Samuel was a fan of the American TV show, *Alf*. He said that his brother was an *Alf* fan too when they were younger. Christina had told me during our first evening with the family that she was quite a fan of the *Gilmore Girls* TV show.

Samuel then told us he'd drop us at our hotel, on his way to bring Marla back to her parent's home just outside the city.

We had a 7:53 train to catch the next morning so we were up and out early. On Christmas Day, Seraphina and Samuel had helped us to reserve our tickets as well as select our specific seats on the train. We stood at the appointed spot at the appointed time and got on the train. Then we found our reserved seats (or so we thought) and got beverages from the attendant going through the aisle with a beverage cart. We settled in for the four and a half hour train ride to Nuremberg and waited for the conductor to come by to look at our tickets.

At the next stop, several other passengers got on and entered our car, including a young man who appeared to be college-aged and an elderly German couple. The young man sat several rows ahead of us, but the older couple stood in the aisle next to our seats and proceeded to speak to us in German, their faces and tone of voice appearing to be rather unhappy. We asked if they spoke English, and they did not, but they evidently believed that we were in their reserved seats. But Seraphina and Samuel had reserved our seats, so there had to have been some mistake.

Since they couldn't speak English and we couldn't speak enough German to understand them, Eric asked the college-aged young man if he could assist us with understanding each other. The man agreed and said that the couple was saying we were in their reserved seats. We showed the young man our tickets that Seraphina had printed out for us on her printer, and then he told us that we were in the wrong train car. We had the seat numbers right, but we were one car off. So we apologized to the elderly couple, thanked the young man, and picked up our items to relocate to the train car behind us. Had the conductor come by before then, he or she would have immediately told us of our error.

We arrived in Nuremberg. Angelina's train arrival time came, but there were platforms on different levels and we weren't sure exactly where to wait for her. After a few minutes of no luck finding her, Eric and I decided to split up and each take a level to try to look for her. Even though he had never seen her before, she remembered seeing some photos of him that I had sent to her in years gone by, and she recognized him as soon as she saw him. She walked right up to him and asked, "Are you Martha's husband?" He affirmed that he was, and they came down the stairs to the warmer station area where I had been looking for her. It was so good to see Angelina again after over three decades.

She had booked herself a hotel room so that she didn't have to head right back home that same day, and we all ventured off to locate her hotel. Eric asked her if she wanted to grab a taxi to take us to her hotel, but she waved off that idea and said she didn't think it would be very far to walk. So we walked and talked, while she looked at her map, eventually turning it over to Eric as we gals were chatting more than paying attention to where we should go.

Her phone's GPS was only helpful up to a point, so she ended up asking a few passers-by for assistance. Unfortunately, none of the people she asked provided her any helpful information, even though she asked them in German. Angelina's husband was German and she spoke German, but evidently with an Austrian accent or dialect, according to what people had told her over the years. Our interactions with strangers that day, without our family members present, weren't nearly as friendly as when we had family with us.

After much walking, we finally located her hotel and rested in her room for a while. She gave us a container of Austrian chocolates for our trip home, but we were getting hungry and all sampled some immediately. After an hour or so we headed out to find some dinner. We walked some more and went inside the walls of the "old city" section, and quickly found an appropriate restaurant. We had a nice meal and conversation. It seemed as if it had merely been approximately three years ago that Angelina and I had lived in the same college dorm, instead of three decades.

Eric spotted a cigar store across the street from the restaurant, so after we ate we visited it. But unfortunately Eric was not able to get any of the Cuban cigars like Rolf had given him last week. By that point it was getting dark, so instead of attempting to do much sight-seeing, we headed back toward Angelina's hotel to visit with her some more in her room. Because Eric and I already had a beautiful hotel room back in Cologne, our reserved return train ticket was for that evening. Angelina seemed disappointed that we wouldn't be able to do some sight-seeing all together in the morning but understood. We hugged Angelina good-bye and wished her a nice morning of sightseeing there in Nuremberg the next day.

After so much walking that day, we were glad to have a taxi take us to the station. Since the few benches were already filled with other people, we sat on the floor waiting for our train. I went to the rest room and when I got back, Eric was now standing and had a sour look on his face. Evidently the *Polizei* (police) had come by and told Eric that he had to stand up. To discourage vagrants, the police swept the station regularly and made sure that people were not sitting or lying down on the floor. Eric and I both thought it was strange that an out-of-town visitor could not rest their legs by sitting on the floor for a few minutes, but pigeons were allowed to fly in and out of the station at will, and could even hang out near the food court areas. And we had seen people bringing dogs into the area earlier in the day also. Here in Germany, there were fewer rules about animals and sanitary food conditions, but more rules about people sitting on the train station floors. Thankfully we were soon able to embark on our train trip back to Cologne. We were grateful for our comfortable hotel bed when we finally got back to our room.

CHAPTER 24

December 30, 2015

We were glad to sleep in a bit later the next morning, and thankfully Christina and Timothy had scheduled a later start time for our trip with them to Aachen, a city where they had lived for several years when they were first married. It was a beautiful sunny day, and although chilly it still seemed mild compared to New England's days at the end of December. We passed by splendid scenery from our high seats on the double decker train that morning. I was very happy to hear my niece tell us that they were considering vacationing in the United States in 2017 and if their plans materialized, they would include some time visiting us in Maine.

Once our train arrived at our destination, we walked past a lovely courtyard of buildings with many shops and businesses. We also walked past a building where symphonies and musical theater productions are held. We continued on and pretty soon we arrived at the famed area of the hot springs, where many different kings had chosen to reside long ago due to the plentiful hot water. A sulfur smell filled the air, and we each held our fingers under the stream of warm spring water flowing from the Elisen-brunnen fountain. This tourist attraction was charming, and we were just a few of the numerous visitors present on this nice day.

Then we wandered through the nearby farmer's market which included several fish stands, and I learned that neither Christina nor Timothy eat fish. Upon hearing this, and the fact that their family might visit us in Maine in a couple of years, I hoped that I might get a chance to show them (or at least their little daughter Sonja) how delicious fresh Maine seafood is.

Then we all continued to walk to the ElisenGalerie, which was a very nice shopping mall with a beautiful glass atrium at the top. By this time we were hungry, and Eric and I were thankful for a little rest. Here we ate lunch at a cafeteria style food court area. After all of our walking this morning and all the walking we had done in Nuremberg the previous day, Eric was quite tired. After he finished eating, he ended up resting his head on Christina's shoulder. She smiled and rested her head on the top of Eric's head, and I took their photo from across the table. This made my heart sing. It was a very cute and familial moment.

Once we had finished eating and felt more rested, we headed out onto the streets of Aachen once again. Soon we arrived at the Aachen Dom, a much smaller cathedral than the Kölner Dom near our hotel. I took several pictures of the beautiful architecture of the building, as well as a photo of Christina and Timothy standing next to the miniature replica of the handsome structure. Then we went inside but I tucked my camera away as Christina told me that photographs were not allowed.

Supposedly the emperor Charlemagne was buried in Aachen Cathedral. The doors of the building have bronze animal heads with openings for the mouths. Legend indicates if a visitor can stick their finger into the opening and successfully pull their finger out unharmed, the visitor will have good luck. To me the heads looked like lions but supposedly they were wolves. Anyway, on our way out, Eric had to try it and I took his photo with his finger in the wolf's "mouth." He was doubtful of the potential good luck to come his way, but he went along with this custom.

Next we headed to the area where the government buildings were located. These looked much more church-like than the government buildings back home. Christina particularly wanted to take our photo standing at the top of the entryway steps to the courthouse. After walking around this area some more, both Eric and I were feeling the need to sit down and rest. So we went into a nearby restaurant and ordered beverages.

After Timothy finished his drink, he said he was going to go look for something and he grabbed his coat and left. I took advantage of the time when Eric went to the rest room to discuss a personal issue with Christina. I inquired of my niece if Marla had passed on to her my message from when Samuel and Marla had visited us, that if any of my women relatives noticed any unusual female symptoms, they should go to a doctor right away. Christina responded that yes Marla had shared this information with her, and she appreciated the warning.

Soon Timothy returned and said to his wife that his quest was successful, but they were keeping secret from us what that quest entailed. Then we all put on our coats and followed him to our next destination, which turned out to be a very well-regarded cigar shop. Thanks to Timothy's determination to locate this store, and perhaps with a bit of the good luck from the wolf's/lion's head on the door of the Aachen Cathedral, Eric was able to purchase six of the exact same type of Cuban cigars that he had received from my brother at Christmas. My husband was tickled to get more, but was also a bit nervous as to whether they would be found and confiscated by the customs officials when we arrived back home.

Then it was time to head back to the train station to go back to Cologne, so that we could meet up with Samuel, Erik, and Aida, for a late supper. It seemed to Eric and me that Timothy was trying to distract us by pointing out odd decorations, and we noticed that Christina had slipped away. We were right. Once we all got on the train and settled in for the hour-long ride back, Christina gave us some spicy-gingerbread-type cookies which she had just purchased. These were her favorites and only available here in Aachen, she said.

We were all rather tired at this point and were more subdued on this train ride home than we had been on the morning one. The hour on the train made for a good time to decompress from our Aachen sight-seeing, and transition to an evening out with my nephews. But then Christina got a text message from Erik that pregnant Aida was not feeling well and so they would not be joining us for dinner that evening as planned. But Samuel would still be joining us, which I was pleased to hear. Soon we were back at the Cologne station, and we bid farewell to my niece and her husband and thanked them for the lovely tour around their beloved city.

Eric and I went to our hotel room and soon Samuel messaged me that he was arriving shortly. I messaged him back our room number so he could come upstairs to meet us. He was impressed with how nice our room was, and I told him that we had been pleasantly surprised as well when we saw it. Then he asked us if we had a preference of what we ate, and Eric said that he would love to try to get in at the Hard Rock Café there in Cologne if possible. So we three headed off to that location, walking along the Rhine River to get there.

I was surprised at how cold it was that evening, even with my "Yankee blood." The wind and moisture from the flowing river must have contributed to the chilly night air. However, the festive lights and decorations around the area made the cold walk worth it. We even walked over a little footbridge that had a lighted skating rink running next to and underneath it, with many skaters using it that evening.

Finally, we arrived at the Hard Rock Café but found out that there would be an hour long wait for a table. Eric was satisfied with simply purchasing a T-shirt and a couple of other small souvenir items in their gift shop. We then walked a short distance to a large restaurant and were able to be seated upstairs in their huge dining area. A live band was playing that evening, which made it very difficult to hear each other to have a conversation. But the food was delicious.

Because of the noise, it was hard to hear what Samuel was saying to us, but I did catch that he said he had been looking at his photos from his and Marla's trip to visit Eric and me in Maine a year ago now. And how much it had meant to him that we had welcomed them and showed him where his grandfather was buried and many places that were important in his grandfather's life. It seemed like Samuel was getting nostalgic and speaking from the heart, and I was sorry that the loud environment of the restaurant interfered with my ability to receive the entire message my nephew was trying to convey. But I was able to get the gist of what he was saying, and I was grateful for what I could understand.

By the time we finished our meal, we were all pretty tired as Samuel had worked all day, so he walked us back to our hotel and we hugged him good-bye, knowing that he'd be heading to Hamburg the next day to spend New Year's with his girlfriend Marla. The next time we'd see him would be for our trip to the airport to fly back home.

CHAPTER 25

December 31, 2015

This day was scheduled to be our alone time for most of the day, with an evening New Year's Eve celebration with many of my family members. So we spent a relaxed morning sleeping in and having breakfast in our room. We had done more walking in the past week than we had in years. But I was loving having my newfound family members show us sights they selected to share with us.

Today we could go exploring the city of Cologne on our own, up to a point. There was a museum of historical Nazi documents that Eric was interested in seeing, but it was closed for the long holiday weekend. We wandered around the city and did some more souvenir shopping. We even roamed around the Cologne train station because it was like a mall there with many shopping options. There was even a McDonald's, and Eric thought he might be able to get a mid-afternoon coffee that would be more like his beloved black coffee at home. Every coffee he had in this country seemed to have some foam on the top of it, and he was not a fan of the foam. But alas, even the train station's McDonald's coffee had some foaminess to it as well.

I debated about whether to purchase a dress for tonight's festivities, which would include dinner out and watching fireworks. But Aida had warned me to dress warmly, and so I felt that wearing nice but warm slacks with a crisp white blouse and nice sweater under my coat for additional warmth outdoors would be fine. Besides, none of the dresses I saw in the store windows jumped out at me as something I really wanted.

Before too long, Eric wanted to head back to our room. As the evening approached, either his McDonald's coffee or something else was not agreeing with him, and he decided he'd be best served to skip the planned evening festivities. I asked him if he minded if I still went out with my brother and family. He said that was fine and he would probably be going to bed early anyway.

I got ready for the evening and headed down to the lobby to meet my family. Soon Rolf, Erik, Seraphina, and Aida arrived, having taken the train in to the city. I could tell that I was the least dressed-up of our group, and I started to wonder if my decision not to purchase a new dress earlier in the day had been correct. But as we walked to the restaurant where my brother had made our dinner reservations, I was glad that I was wearing warm slacks as it was quite chilly with a breeze.

Erik explained to me that the restaurant we were going to was extremely old, built in the 1500s. My brother said something loudly for our group to hear, and everyone else laughed, and then Erik told me that my brother had said we need not be concerned about the food because it is not from the 1500s. I laughed and once again thought of my dad's sense of humor.

As it turns out, my husband was not the only member of our New Year's Eve dinner group who was feeling a bit under the weather. Lorraine had messaged her dad that she was not feeling very well either, and she and Dietrich would not be joining us as planned.

We arrived at the restaurant and as scheduled, met up with a long-time girlfriend of Seraphina's and her British husband. This British friend of Rolf's and Seraphina's, James, was a big car enthusiast, and my brother and sister-in-law felt that he and my husband Eric would enjoy talking with each other in English about cars. So this gentleman was rather disappointed when he learned that Eric would not be joining us for dinner. He had evidently been looking forward to discussing automobile topics with my husband.

The hostess showed us the way to our table, which was downstairs in what appeared to be a nicely decorated but very old cellar. According to the information on the menu written in English which I was provided,

"The cellar still contains stone structure that was left over from the Roman city wall." And it appeared to me that we were seated in that extremely old section.

Rolf told James that I had been learning to speak some German, and his response was "Well then, we will have to speak just German this evening." And I shook my head no and responded "Nein, ich kann sie nicht verstehen," which is "No, I cannot understand you." They all laughed and my brother smiled at me and put his arm around me. I think it surprised them when I said something correctly in German... at least I believe that I said it correctly.

We reviewed the menu, and I chose to forego the cream soup appetizer that the others selected. And I decided to go with the pork chop rather than the oxen casserole or other exotic-sounding dishes. Although there was quite a long wait for our food to be served, it was very good, and several of the others enjoyed coffee and dessert afterward. The conversation continued until nearly 11 p.m., when we left the restaurant and walked back toward the Kölner Dom (Cologne Cathedral) plaza.

What surprised me was how many people in the crowded area were shooting off both small firecrackers and full-fledged fireworks. Since they were so close, they were very loud. I walked with Erik and Aida, and I was close enough to Aida to be able to holler in her ear that this was even louder than being at a NASCAR race.

As we approached the cathedral's plaza, it became extremely crowded. Aida kindly linked her arm with mine to prevent us from getting separated as we squeezed our way through the mass of people, many of them young men. I tried to stick as close to Aida as possible, holding on to her arm with mine, and holding my purse close to my torso with my other arm. I most certainly did not want to get separated from my family in this strange and rather scary environment.

The police were trying to disperse the large crowd, some of whom were still setting off firecrackers despite the mass of people. We saw a couple of men loudly questioning the policemen who had stopped them from proceeding, asking why they couldn't go this way and saying that their brother had planned to meet them in this direction. Aida led me away from this confrontation in case it escalated beyond just loud words.

Finally, Rolf, James and his wife, Erik, Aida, and I all made it to a less crowded area at the far edge of the plaza. I was relieved to meet back up with Rolf and Erik.

But where was Seraphina?

We looked around but she was nowhere to be found in this huge crowd. She had somehow gotten separated from Rolf and their friends. A few minutes passed and then Rolf started trying to call and text her, to no avail. Then Erik started texting Seraphina's phone also. Several more minutes passed, and although both men tried to appear that everything was fine, I could tell that they were both rather worried about her, as was I.

Finally after about ten more minutes, Seraphina must have received and seen their texts as to where specifically we all were and she joined us, much to our collective relief. She said that she was fine, and I told her that I was very glad she was OK.

In Germany, fireworks can only be legally purchased on the couple of days leading up to New Year's. Many people in the area of the Cologne Cathedral seemed to have unleashed their pent-up desires to set off these explosives.

Erik told me that usually this plaza is not nearly as congested on New Year's Eve. Although we did not know it at the time, the police received many complaints regarding the happenings in that area that evening. It was undeniably a rowdy night there. Once Seraphina had rejoined our group, we headed toward a deserted bridge area to get away from the massive crowd, and so that Erik and Rolf could safely set off the fireworks they had brought.

In the relative quiet of where we now were, Rolf opened a bottle of champagne. It was nearly midnight, and Seraphina passed out little plastic cups and everyone had a toast to 2016. Then Rolf gave each of us a sparkler to waive.

There was no countdown to midnight like the American custom, and no kissing at midnight. But we could tell that the stroke of midnight was upon us as the number of firecrackers exploding in the general vicinity rapidly increased. Erik lighted the firecrackers he and Rolf had brought, and Erik seemed to be especially enjoying setting them off.

The only fireworks at midnight were those which had been purchased by individuals and thus were relatively small ones. There was no big fireworks display put on by the city or sponsored by the government, at least not here in Cologne. After Erik set off the last of the firecrackers, we decided to walk to our hotel to warm up as it was getting quite chilly after spending the last hour or more outside.

Although the hotel's lounge was rather crowded, we were somehow able to get a table where all of us could sit down and have a drink. After we placed our drink orders, Rolf and Erik noticed their phones had messages indicating the police had shut down the Cologne train station due to the unruly crowd near there. They thought it was good that we all were hanging out in the hotel for a while, to wait for the police to disperse the crowd and get the train station back open so that my family members could get back home.

We made more small talk for a while as everyone sipped their drinks. My brother and nephew kept checking their phones to see if there was any update on the train station. Before long it was nearly 1:30 and Erik told me that they had decided to try to get a taxi to take them all back to their cars at the train station near their homes. We bid each other good-night and Happy New Year.

I took the elevator up to our room. Eric was snoring as I entered, and I tip-toed around as I got ready for bed so as not to wake him. I was surprised he was able to sleep as I could still hear a number of firecrackers being set off fairly nearby. I was glad I had packed ear plugs; they came in handy that night.

CHAPTER 26

January 1 and 2, 2016

The next morning I slept in since I had been out so late the night before, and Eric was glad for a leisurely morning. Thankfully, he was feeling better and we decided to go downstairs to the dining area to try their New Year's Day breakfast buffet. We enjoyed sampling the wide variety of food options, and after eating Eric went up to our room to retrieve something he had forgotten. I remained at the table and people-watched, reflecting on what a wonderful time we have had on this trip, and that today was our last full day in Germany.

After Eric returned to the table, we chatted and relaxed a bit more and then decided we should start packing for our trip home the next morning. After an hour or so of packing, we decided to do a bit more exploring of Cologne. As we strolled around the mostly deserted section of the city, we saw many empty beer bottles strewn about and signs of the many firecrackers and larger fireworks that had been set off the night before.

We walked over to the Hohenzollern Bridge with the thousands of locked padlocks on it. A custom is for couples to purchase a padlock, get their names engraved on that lock, secure it to a spot on the wire fence, which is up against the side of the bridge, and then drop the key into the Rhine River below to symbolize that the couple's love will go on forever.

We wandered around some more and saw some concert posters for events taking place in the city in the upcoming summer season. Eric noticed a poster for his favorite group, Deep Purple, and they were scheduled to give a concert in Krefeld in July. I said no, we would not be returning all the way here for that concert. He settled for a photo of him standing next to the poster. We saw an empty tourist boat on the river, and assumed that their busiest times were in warmer weather. Then we decided to head back to our hotel room to warm up.

In the mid-afternoon, Rolf and Seraphina, Erik and Aida, and Christina, Timothy, and little Sonja all came to our hotel to spend some more time with us on our last day in their country. Christina and family were the last to arrive, and when I saw little Sonja walking ahead of her parents as they entered the hotel lobby, I knelt down on one knee and opened my arms wide to greet her. I was very happy that she took my cue and ran into my arms to give me a hug.

We all headed out to the Cologne Cathedral plaza, and by this time there were more people wandering around that area. Rolf stopped a young man to ask if he'd mind taking a photo of all of us standing on the steps with the cathedral behind us, and he agreed.

Afterward, Aida handed me a small wrapped item and said it was for Eric and me from all of them. I unwrapped it and it was a bright red padlock with "Martha & Eric" engraved on the front, and "& your German family" engraved on the back. I was very pleased that they did this for us. Then we all had to walk over to where the many locks were on the fence next to the bridge, to locate a good spot to put it. There were so many locks already there, it was challenging to find a space, but we finally did.

My brother's children suggested that Eric and I drop the key into the river, but Eric thought it would be even more meaningful to have Rolf and I drop the key into the water instead. So that's what we did. It was quite windy so close to the river, and any photos taken at this point had my hair whipping all around. But I didn't care; it was an amazing moment.

Then we wandered toward the area where there were a couple of restaurants, and since it was so windy and chilly, we wanted to see if we could locate a place where we could all go inside, warm up and have a little something to drink and possibly eat as well. However, on this major holiday, every restaurant that we stopped at informed us that they already had people waiting for tables and with the size of our party (eight adults and one child) it would take a long time for us to wait. So we kept on walking and trying other restaurants, but to no avail.

Finally, we decided to head back to our hotel and inquire if we could get some food and beverages there, even though the lounge area was closed for the holiday. Seraphina's job evidently requires her to negotiate things on a regular basis, and she was very good at persuading the person in charge of their food service to allow the nine of us to hang out in an out-of-the-way section at the back of their large lobby, and have "room service" provided to us there (and charged to our room). We were told that the food options would be limited, and we were fine with that. We just wanted to be able to spend time together talking, warming up, and having a little something to eat and drink. It worked out great. We enjoyed hanging out and the waiter even brought some crayons and a coloring book for Sonja to keep her occupied. It was quieter in this spot than probably any of the crowded restaurants would have been anyway.

Eric and I enjoyed spending this last hour or so with many of my new family members. After a while, little Sonja started to get antsy and began running around a bit, and so Christina and Timothy said their good-byes. Shortly after they left, Rolf and Seraphina and Erik and Aida all got ready to leave as well. Eric and I thanked Seraphina for getting the hotel to allow us this visiting time together, and Rolf said he would come to the airport in the morning to see us off. Erik and Aida said their good-byes, and we thanked them for their hospitality. I wished Aida good luck with the impending birth of their first child in a couple of months, and Eric told her as they hugged goodbye that she'll make a wonderful mother. Then Eric and I headed up to our room to finish packing and hit the sack early since we'd have an early flight.

The next morning we rose *very* early, finished packing, and headed down to the lobby to check out. We told the desk clerk how pleased we were with the staff who had made our visiting time with my family last evening so perfect.

Soon my nephew Samuel came along and smiled as he exited his car, saying "Did someone order VIP shuttle service to the airport?"

On the ride we had a nice chat about our time visiting everyone, and soon we were at the Dusseldorf airport. The three of us went to the coffee shop and my brother arrived shortly thereafter, having taken the train to get there. We chatted a bit more, and then soon it was time for the two of us to go through the line for security to be able to board our plane for Munich.

I hugged both my nephew and my brother and had tears in my eyes as I said good-bye. Samuel said that we would definitely see each other via video chat soon, and now that we'd visited back and forth, it would be easier to do so again moving forward. I hated to say good-bye, and Eric told me, "Oh go ahead and hug 'em again," and so I did. Then we grabbed our carry-on bags and walked to the end of the line for security. We waived as we went through the glass doors that closed behind us, and we were on our way home.

I was *so* grateful that everything on this trip had gone so well.

CHAPTER 27

Conclusion

On the flight home, I basked in the warmth of our experiences over the last twelve days, and I used the numerous hours in the air to scribble in a notebook about the many details I wanted to always remember.

I also felt very appreciative for the wonderful opportunity that had been presented to me. I was thankful that Samuel had searched the internet and had found my mother's obituary with my dad's and my names in it. It still seems very ironic that my mother had been the barrier between Daddy, me, and our family in Germany yet it was her obituary that was the conduit to bring us together.

I was grateful that Samuel had reached out to me when he did, and that he had easily located my work email address on the internet. I was appreciative that I had a job which readily publicized that email address, so he could access it. And I was very thankful that Eric and I had both the physical and financial health to be able to make this trip.

And now that I have a good relationship with these new relatives, I can connect with them regularly through various electronic communication methods, as well as via snail mail.

I had no intention of this being our one and only time seeing these new family members, and evidently many of them felt the same way. As Christina and Timothy had told us on our day trip with them to Aachen, they planned to bring little Sonja to visit us in 2017, and thankfully that plan came to fruition. Their family came to the United States in June 2017, when Sonja was five and a half years old, and spent some time vacationing in New York City. Then they came to spend several days visiting us before returning back to New York City to fly home.

My brother wanted to show me where he had grown up, in Berlin, and Eric and I were very interested to see this. So, in May of 2018, we flew back to Germany and spent time visiting with my family again. During our first visit in 2015, Erik's wife Aida was pregnant; now their little girl was two years old. We were able to meet her on this trip. Seeing my brother's two granddaughters playing together at his home with many family members nearby was such a joy for me.

On this trip, some of our days included visits with not only my family but additional in-laws: Aida's parents and Marla's parents. By happy coincidence, we were there the weekend of the annual twenty-four hours of Nürburgring auto race. Samuel, along with Marla's father who had been an engineer with an auto race team, brought us to the track to see part of this race. Eric was in seventh heaven. Marla's dad got to reconnect with some people he hadn't seen in a few years, and I really enjoyed seeing Eric so happy and in his element at this race. He had now seen this famous racetrack when it was deserted right before Christmas, as well as when it was at its busiest.

The next day, Rolf and Christina took us by train to Berlin. We four stayed in a hotel in that city for a couple of days, seeing the sights. Having my brother show us places of importance to him, including three different apartment buildings where he had lived while growing up, was very meaningful for me. He also showed us the grave of his aunt, who had died several years ago, and who had been very important in his life after the death of his mother.

After we returned to Lippstadt from Berlin, we were invited to a birthday party luncheon for Rose, the mother of my two nephews and eldest niece. In addition to Rose's children and grandchildren, my brother and his wife, Aida's parents, and Marla's parents all attended. It was a very festive event, and we were so pleased to be included. This whole trip to Germany was fantastic also.

Christina and her family scheduled another trip to visit us in summer 2020. However, the whole world was battling the COVID-19 virus that year and naturally their trip had to be cancelled. I hoped to spend my brother's 75th birthday with him in the fall of 2021, but unfortunately issues surrounding COVID and significant flooding in that area in late summer caused us to decide to postpone another trip there. Hopefully, we can spend his 76th birthday with him in 2022 instead.

Some minor health issues make me unsure if my brother will ever return to the United States, unfortunately. I don't know if I will ever have the opportunity to show my brother some of the people and places of importance to me here. But that's OK. I'm grateful for the connection that we have made, and that we have been warmly welcomed both times we've visited my family there in Germany. And I expect that we will have multiple opportunities to show my brother's children various places of interest here in the future. Erik and Aida are already mentioning a possible visit in 2022 or 2023.

I feel certain that my father would have been very happy that Eric and I travelled to Germany to meet Rolf and his family. I feel that he would also be proud of me that I had spent so much time and effort to learn German so that I could talk with Rolf a little bit without someone always translating everything for us. And I'm sure Daddy would be pleased that Rolf and his family had spent so much time and effort to get to know us and provide us with so many marvelous experiences during our visits.

I also believe my dad would be very happy that now, in addition to having two great-granddaughters, he also has a great-grandson. Erik and Aida had a son in 2020, during the pandemic, and his name also begins with the letter L. I'm sure that Daddy would be very proud if he were here.

I believe that my mother would be OK with my developing a relationship with my dad's offspring, because she is not here to see it. I still have some mixed feelings about my parents having kept this secret from me, and about my father having cheated on my mother. And I feel certain that my mother was the barrier against my dad connecting with his son and grandchildren. I wish she had let me know about my brother. But I'm very happy that I now have this wonderful extended family.

There will be many questions for which I will never find answers... like how my father's and Gretchen's relationship came about. Daddy's army yearbook stated: "The present duties are guarding prisoners and loading lumber... "

I can assume that guarding prisoners was evidently a very important part of his experience serving overseas. This is because Samuel's email that included the first pieces of my father's 1951 letter stated: *"In fact my Grandma met him in a city named Deggendorf in bavaria. I dind't now that so far. My Grandma was interned there. She was brought to Deggendorf from somewhere in Italy. I dont now if she met Lawrence Rollins already in Italy or only in Bavaria."*

Thus, my assumption is that he met Gretchen when she was interned— a prisoner, and he was a guard. This would have made their relationship even more forbidden. And I do believe that they had a real loving relationship, based on the letters that were obviously written.

How were they able to communicate when they met, since Rolf said his mother did not speak English? I'm guessing that my dad had learned enough German words to make himself understood. I'm also guessing that my father knew when he was sent back home to the United States that Gretchen was pregnant, but I do not know for sure. And how was Gretchen able to obtain my parents' mailing address in order to send my father letters, which my mother intercepted? I will never know.

I am very grateful for Eric accompanying me on these trips, as it was much less scary to go on my first flights abroad with my husband than if I had gone by myself.

My strong desire to be healthy now stems from wanting to travel to the weddings of Samuel and Marla (I hope within the next couple of years, now that they are engaged), and perhaps even the weddings of my little grandnieces many years from now. Sonja is already starting to learn English in school, and I look forward to communicating with these children in English as they grow up.

Before learning about my German family, I had toyed with the idea of someday visiting Paris. But I never thought it would actually come to pass. And if anyone had told me in 2013 or earlier that I would visit Germany and other European countries, I would have told them they were dead wrong. But having visited Germany, and Ireland for a brief two-day stop on our way home in 2018, and learned a bit about each of these other countries, I have a new appreciation for certain things.

Traveling to other countries helps show the traveler that American society's expectations are not necessarily universal worldwide. Naturally, showing respect for others' customs, especially when in their country, is very important. It shows courtesy. Traveling opens people up to other points of view, and other ways of doing things.

Also, coming home helped me appreciate some things we take for granted here, like being able to visit the graves of my parents and grandparents and even great-grandparents for as long as I live. I believe I am more open-minded now, as well as more appreciative, than before our travel away from North America. Eric and I hope to visit Switzerland and France when we take other trips to visit my family in the coming years.

This true story is proof that one never knows what might lie just around the next corner of his or her life. You just never know when you wake up in the morning what the day will bring. It might provide an opportunity to dramatically improve your life, *if* you are willing to seize the possibilities.

ACKNOWLEDGMENTS

Janis Hennessey, for her invaluable assistance with editing and proofreading

Marshall Hudson, for his wonderful suggestions for edits and improvements to my first draft

Ericka McIntyre, for her professional editing

Jessica Eslinger, for her professional proofreading

Clare Finney, for designing the cover and interior

Jane Friedman, for her "How to Self-Publish Your Book" video workshop and resources

My nephew, "Samuel Graf," who reached out to me and informed me of my German family

And my husband, "Eric Levallee," for his support, both during my adventure and my time writing about it

REFERENCES

245 Engineer Combat Battalion – Its History and Achievements 1943 – 1945. Printed by Knorr & Hirth, Munich of Bavaria. Editors: Cpl. Clifford M. Anderson and T/5 Paul D. Spofford, A Company; T/5 Andrew W. O'Rourke and T/5 George B. Hance, B Company; Cpl. Michael J. McGrail Jr. and Cpl. Joseph N. Seifert, Jr., C Company; and Cpl. Edgar G. Carson and T/5 Thomas F. Mausolff, H&S Company.